CHOOSING
A WORD PROCESSOR

—— CHOOSING ——
A WORD PROCESSOR

Phillip I. Good

RESTON PUBLISHING COMPANY, INC.
A Prentice-Hall Company
RESTON, VIRGINIA 22090

Library of Congress Cataloging in Publication Data

Good, Phillip I.
    Choosing a word processor.
    1. Word processing equipment. 2. Word processing
equipment–Purchasing. I. Title.
HF5548.2.G5965 1982   681'.6   82-21525
ISBN 0-8359-0761-9
ISBN 0-8359-0760-0 (pbk.)

Published by: RESTON PUBLISHING COMPANY, INC.
            A Prentice-Hall Company
            RESTON, VIRGINIA 22090

Portions of this book appeared in somewhat different form in
DataCast, the Laboratory Computer Letter, Popular Computing,
and Small Business Computing.

Interior design and production by: Jack Zibulsky
Cover design by: Debbie Balboni

Printed in the United States of America

TABLE OF
CONTENTS

PART 3   HARDWARE

PART 4   THE DECISION

PART 5   COMPARISON TABLES

APPENDIXES

PREFACE

In mid 1980, I bought a microcomputer for my own word processing needs. Now, almost three years later, I realize that I have had to replace almost every component of the system including the software. I don't want this to happen to you. The purpose of this book is to help you to buy smart, and to select a word processing system that is right for your needs, now and three years from now.

On the next page you will find a master check list. Follow it carefully. It will guide you through the selection process with a minimum of effort on your part and a maximum of savings in capital and energy.

The master check list is just one of twelve check lists in this book. Complete each one. Use the comparison tables at the end of the text. By doing so, you will select the system that is best for you—the very first time around.

Phillip I. Good

CHECK LIST

MASTER CHECK LIST

ITEMS 1-100. Know your application(s). Learn what computers can do, then decide what you want the computer to do for you now and in the next two to three years. Complete the application check list on page 16.

101. Do you need a word processor? Complete the check list on page 12.

102. Select your word-processing software. Let the software determine the system. Complete the software selection check list on page 31. Consult head-to-head comparison tables on pages 138 to 173.

103. Choose your computer. Complete the hardware check list on page 85.

104. Specify additional operating systems, disk drives, printers or terminals that do not come with the computer. Be sure you see printers and terminals in operation before you buy. Complete the check list on pages 92, 99, and 113.

WARNING: Be sure ALL components can be serviced locally.

105. Order the equipment and software. Negotiate the sales contract. Specify payment only on successful and complete installation. Be sure the contract provides for both training and maintenance. Complete the contract check list in Appendix 1.

106. Don't forget stands, tables, extension cords, floppy disks, diskette holder, ribbons, forms, modems, etc. Complete the miscellaneous check list in Appendix 2.

PART 1

INTRODUCTION

CHAPTER 1

Benefits
for Everyone

A little over a year and a half ago, I was walking out of an office supply store, the owner of a brand-new electronic typewriter. Minutes later, I walked back into the store, returned the typewriter and retrieved my check from the startled shopkeeper. I had fallen victim to computer fever.

Walking to my car, I had happened to pass by the window of a newly opened computer store. A sign said, *Word processor for sale.* The price of the computer, $3000, struck me as more than I wanted to pay. But if it would take the place of two typewriters, as the store manager assured me it would, maybe I could come out ahead.

As it happens, I did and I didn't. I was able to get far more writing done than I could with a typewriter alone—almost one hundred percent more. The copy was far more polished, far more professional, than anything my firm had produced in the past. As an added bonus, my desk-top word processor served as calculator, tax accountant and financial record keeper. But I didn't do it all for three thousand dollars.

First, the small matrix printer included in the initial offer produced poor quality print. There was no way it could serve as a "second typewriter." The "free" dot-matrix printer had to be replaced almost immediately with a letter quality printer at a cost of $2500—almost what I had paid for the system in the first place.

Second, my computer was an off-brand, soon destined to pass from the scene. I have parts today only through the lucky break of acquiring a second identical model at a bankruptcy sale, and service only through a chance encounter with a young man who combines mechanical and electronic abilities with a willing spirit.

Third, I had to pay an extra $400 for the word-processing *software*. Actually, I was fortunate. I could have purchased a computer for which there was absolutely no software available.

Of course, all this was months ago. I have since had the opportunity to examine twenty brands of computers, and twice that number of word-processing packages. And I've learned some very valuable lessons along the way, lessons that can help you acquire the wordprocessing capability you need, without trauma and without unnecessary expense.

I now know enough to **buy service first.** I know I should buy the software *before* I buy the computer. You'll find these rules in our very first checklist. Incidentally, this book is full of check lists for two important reasons. First and foremost, I don't want you to waste time and money because you bought the wrong product. Second, different people have different needs. I want your word-processing system to be right for you.

At the conclusion of each chapter, you'll be asked to fill out a check list with your own requirements and your own needs. Write them in the space provided; don't trust them to memory. Your requirements, not a sales representative's, should be the basis of your purchase decision.

I want you to buy smart. Buying smart means that you will buy for *your* applications, not mine, not a sales representative's, and not the store owner's. There are twelve check lists in this book. Once completed, they will summarize your needs. Take them with you when you shop. There are several pages of head-to-head comparisons at the end of this book. Use them to finalize your choices. When you are finished, this will be as much your book as mine.

The very first question you should ask yourself is, "Do I need a word processor?" A discussion of this topic follows in Chapter Two.

CHAPTER 2

Why Buy a Word Processor?

I once had a boss who had an iron clad rule that a document could only be retyped once. I can understand his concern, particularly now that I own my own business. His unit had limited secretarial resources and he wanted to make the most effective use of them. But the net result was that the letters and reports that left our department were a continual source of embarrassment. Even our memos showed a lack of polish and concern.

Secretaries cost money. But so do sales representatives. Because I run a very small business, most of my selling is done by letter. Those letters may be my only contact with the customer. They have to look their best. If you correspond with the public on a regular basis, you will want a word processor.

On a typical morning, I may get out four letters to four different customers. The letters are more or less the same with minor modifications to fit the needs of the individual customer. I dictate the first letter from scratch, but the other three start out almost as carbon copies of the first. Usually, I can think of one or two additional selling points as I go, and maybe I'll delete a line or two that detracts from the rest. By the time I'm finished, I realize I ought to go back to the very first letter and modify it as well. And I do go back, easily and without guilt, because I don't have a secretary, I have a word processor.

Almost every business has four or five standard letters which it routinely sends out with perhaps one or two modifications. When I worked for a large corporation, it was typical for me to say, "Use the first paragraph from the Jones letter, take the next two from the manual, and I'll add a line or two at the end." You can give exactly the same instructions to a word processor, and you won't have to pay for retyping the material or for time spent searching through file cabinets.

Do You Need a Word Processor?

You need a word processor if you want your correspondence to look professional—no typos, no type-overs and white-outs, no misspellings, and proper spacing. You need a word processor if you frequently need extra copies. Each copy or revision can be typed without error at 225 words per minute, about three times the speed of a fast and very accurate typist.

You need a word processor when your typists are working overtime, or if you find it difficult to get the secretarial support you need. You need a word processor if you want personalized mass mailings. You need a word processor if you do repetitive typing—the same report over and over, or monthly reports that turn into quarterly reports and then into an annual summary.

We can think of at least 40 to 50 applications of a word processor in the typical small business—not just correspondence, but inventories, lists, and financial reports. You may be able to think of 15 to 20 more applications. Check your needs against the following check list.

CHECK LIST

CHECK LIST OF USES
FOR YOUR WORD PROCESSOR

Address Book	Master File Guides
Agenda	Memoranda
Agreements	Notes
Appointment Calendar	Notices
Bibliography	Outlines
Books	Organization Charts
Case Histories	Personnel Rosters
Contracts	Plans
Correspondence	Press Releases
Documentation	Programs
Drafts	Recipes
Electronic Mail	Regulations
Filing Guides	Reports
Form Letters	Schedules
Forms	Stories
Formula	Subscriber Lists
Formulations	Supply Inventory
Instructions	Syllabus
Inventory	Tables
Lists	Telephone Log
Mailing Lists	Telephone Messages
Maintenance Records	Telephone Numbers
Manuscripts	Verse

Experienced Users

"I knew I needed a word processor," says Dr. Henry Lee, owner and president of Lee Pharmaceuticals in El Monte, CA. "When my engineers complained that they never got the minutes of one meeting until the next had been held!" If your engineers complain about secretarial delays, do what Henry Lee did. Lee purchased 45 desk-top computers for his firm, one for every two engineers. "Now we get out the reports on time and I think they are better written," says Dr. Lee.

Doug Deitel of Hempel Financial Corporation in Los Angeles, CA, says, "Don't buy a typewriter, buy a word processor." John Crawford, head of a team of civil engineers in Carterville, IL, says, "A word processor is ideal when you have to submit the same survey results ten times to ten different agencies, with just a few minor variations each time."

Just in Passing

We're often asked about electronic typewriters, the same electronic typewriter I almost bought what now seems a century ago. The electronic typewriter with its one line or two line display, and the notorious "magnetic card" typewriter are victims of technology, I'm afraid. The rapid pace of computer technology has rendered these "innovations in office technology" obsolete almost from their inception. I don't even recommend an electronic typewriter for use as a printer—it is far too slow.

In the next few chapters of this book, we'll learn what a word processor can do, and the components it takes to get the job done. You can buy on impulse, or you can buy smart, the topic of the next chapter.

CHECK LIST

DO YOU NEED
A WORD PROCESSOR?

You need a word processor if you have any of the applications in the preceeding check list and

- You want your work to look professional.

   no typos

   no type-overs or white-outs

   proper spelling

   proper spacing

- You require multiple copies or frequent updates.

- Your secretaries are working overtime or you can't get the secretarial help you need.

- You do mass mailings.

- You frequently need to integrate past reports or edit the material of others.

CHAPTER 3

Buy Smart

You can pay $15,000 or more for a sophisticated word processing system like those sold by CPT, Lanier, or NBI. This is not expensive, if your application demands specialized features such as Greek and Latin symbols, or the on-line display of chemical formula and mathematical expressions.

Not everyone needs to spend $15,000. The word processing needs of most smallbusinesses can be met by a $5,000 to $7,000 desk-topomputer, and a $400 combined text editor, printer formatter and mail-merge program like Magic Wand or Spellbinder.

But there are pitfalls. If you buy on the basis of cost alone, you may end up with a system gathering dust in the corner. Or you can buy a nationally advertised system that lacks local support and service. The purpose of this book, and of the check list at the end of each chapter, is to help you to buy the most cost-effective system for your application.

Know Your Application

It's hard to avoid giving way to new computer fever, especially when there are computer stores in practically every shopping mall. Your first steps in selecting a word processing system must be back in your office, detailing the requirements—the how much and the how often—of your application.

Sometimes an independent consultant can help, particularly a consultant who understands your applications as well as computers. But you and your staff will need to work with the consultant to establish your word processing needs now and two or three years in the future.

Go to your existing files. How many letters did you write last year? Do you use form letters? How many times did you rewrite (or retype) each letter on the average?

How many documents will you process a day? What are your principal applications—letters, financial reports, documentary material? How many individuals will need to access the system? How often will you need to enter or update material? How often will you need to print it out? Take time now to answer these questions and more in the following check list. This check list is the beginning of your selection process.

Choose the Software First

The single most important component of a computer system is the software—the instructions that tell a computer to do what you bought it to do in the first place. Your selection of applications software can be severely limited by the operating system and computer that you purchase. Choose your word processing software first. Let your applications determine the software and the computer you purchase.

Among competing software, there is a wider range in speed-of-execution and ease-of-use than there is among competing models of computers. Choose your software with care and read this book and the comparison tables before you buy. Guidelines to software selection are given in Part II of this book in Chapters 4 through 9.

CHECK LIST
KNOW YOUR APPLICATION

1. Know Your Application(s)

   • letters

   • reports

   • ledgers

   • forms

2. Review Your Correspondence

   • Do you have clients you contact repeatedly?

   • Do you plan to use electronic mail?

   • Will you be using standard paragraphs (boilerplate)?

   • Do you often do letters with 2 or more pages?

   • How many letters per day: average?

   maximum?

   • How many copies of each letter?

   • How often do you do mass mailings?

   How many pieces per mailing?

3. Review Your Reports

   • What is the average length of a report?

• What is the longest document?

• How often do you work with documents this large?

• Will you integrate the results of several authors?

• Do your reports include: tables?

indexes?

graphs?

• Do you use multiple columns?

• How many copies of each report?

4. Specify Form of Printed Output

Estimate annual usage of

• Single sheets

letterhead

legal size

custom forms

• Continuous forms

standard size

accounting width

custom forms

labels

Now Choose the Hardware

Once you've selected the software, you can give way for a few moments to new computer fever. You'll find that the computer, at least the central processing unit or computer-on-a-chip, is the least expensive component of your system. In addition to the central processing unit, you are going to need a terminal ($500 to $1000), a printer ($500 to $3000 and more), and mass storage devices ($500 to $2000). We'll consider each of these components, the options, and the alternatives in Part III of this book.

You'll find you'll have to make some big choices—a hobbyist or a professional quality computer, a dot-matrix or a letter-quality printer, etc. We provide check lists that will lead you to the solution that is right for you.

Buy Service First

The need for local, timely service must override all other considerations in hardware selection. Dealers frequently discount older, obsolete models. If you opt for such savings, insist on a discount of at least fifty percent. Then you can buy two units, one to use for spare parts.

Should you buy through the mail? Mail-order prices are cheaper. Shipping costs are usually offset by the savings in sales taxes. The answer is yes but only if you can be assured of local service in and out of warranty.

Here is why. On an average, five percent of all equipment—computers, terminals and printers—is dead on arrival. Removing and replacing each component in its socket might fix the problem—if you know what you're doing, and if you can get at the component. Computer dealers are prepared to make this type of repair. Are you?

Once your system is installed and working correctly, you should have few calls for repairs, though there are as many "lemons" among computers as there are among automobiles. Forestall problems and buy service first.

Incidentally, service can be a negotiable item, even when a dealer will not budge on price. Certain dealers, aware of competition from the mail-order houses, are willing to guarantee four-hour response time service, or reduced rates on postwarranty repairs.

Be Prepared to Compromise

You may need to cycle through the check list at the end of this chapter two or even three times. The software that you select on the first pass may not run on equipment that you can get serviced locally. Don't hesitate to start all over at item number 1. That's what check lists are for. They give you the opportunity to explore possibilities before you've made a commitment.

Order Last

Despite the short-term savings you might get by shopping around, buying a loss leader here and a bargain there, it is probably best to order all your equipment, software as well as hardware, from a single dealer. You will want to negotiate a written contract (verbal promises aren't worth the paper they're written on) and it is probably best to do it once with one dealer and do it right.

From your point of view, the negotiation is a relatively simple affair. You agree to pay a fixed amount of dollars in return for a specific set of equipment. You insist that all promises regarding service, warranties, training, and delivery dates are put in writing. You make payment contingent on "complete" and "satisfactory" installation.

A partial system, one without disk drives or software, will be of little or no use to you. Don't pay if you can't play. "Satisfactory" means that all equipment and software function as warranted when part of an integrated system. The warranties apply only to the technical aspects of performance. Careful planning and attention to detail on your part is required to ensure the system will do the job you want done.

CHECK LIST

MASTER CHECK LIST

ITEMS 1-100. Know your application(s). Learn what computers can do, then decide what you want the computer to do for you now and in the next two to three years. Complete the application check list on page 16.

101. Do you need a word processor? Complete the check list on page 12.

102. Select your word-processing software. Let the software determine the system. Complete the software selection check list on page 31. Consult head-to-head comparison tables on pages 138 to 173.

103. Choose your computer. Complete the hardware check list on page 85.

104. Specify additional operating systems, disk drives, printers or terminals that do not come with the computer. Be sure you see printers and terminals in operation before you buy. Complete the check list on pages 92, 99, and 113.

WARNING: Be sure ALL components can be serviced locally.

105. Order the equipment and software. Negotiate the sales contract. Specify payment only on successful and complete installation. Be sure the contract provides for both training and maintenance. Complete the contract check list in Appendix 1.

106. Don't forget stands, tables, extension cords, floppy disks, diskette holder, ribbons, forms, modems, etc. Complete the miscellaneous check list in Appendix 2.

PART 2
SOFTWARE

CHAPTER 4

Select
Your Software First

The single most important component of your word-processing system is the software—the instructions that tell your computer to do what you bought it to do in the first place. Your computer, your operating system, and your printer can limit your selection of software. Choose your software first. Let your applications determine what computer you purchase.

Among competing software, there is a wider range in speed of execution and ease-of-use than there is among competing brands of computers. Buy your software with care, and consult the comparison tables at the end of this book before you buy.

Know Your Application

The most important rule in software selection is to know your application and buy for your application.

Your first steps in selecting a word-processing system are back in your office, detailing the requirements—the how much and the how often—of your application.

How many documents do you process a day? What are your principal applications—letters, financial reports, documentary material? How many letters did you write last year? Do you use form letters? How many times did you rewrite (or retype) each letter on the average? How often do you need to revise or update reports?

We included these questions and more in the check list at the end of Chapter 3. If you've not yet answered those questions, now is the time to go back and complete the check list.

Understand What The Software Can Do

A smart shopper is a knowledgeable shopper. The four chapters in this section give you insight into the features of the best word-processing software available so that you can be a smart shopper.

Not every software package offers every desirable feature. Review the next few chapters carefully. Note which features are important to you, and mark them on the check lists at the end of each chapter. When you proceed to the actual selection process you'll find most of the work has been done for you.

Order The Manual

The major cost of installing a new system is the time you and your employees invest in learning to use it. Use the material in this book to reduce your choices to one or two packages. Then, order the manuals. The manual is the key to a successful installation.

Usually, the manual can be ordered independent of the software for $25 to $35. In most instances, the amount will be credited should you purchase the complete package.

The manuals you review must be professional. I've reviewed manuals that are almost illegible, and some that have neither a table of contents nor an index.

The manual must speak your language. Good software does not require a specialized knowledge of computers and computer systems. You'll recognize *computerese*. And you should also take offense at a manual that talks down to you.

One of the worst word processors is accompanied by 200 pages of closely compressed text. One of the best has a manual that says what needs to be said in 128 pages devoted mainly to examples and illustrations.

The manual should contain at least six sections:

- a table of contents

- tutorials

- examples

- a reference section

• an index

• a quick reference card

Look in the table of contents for your individual needs. If you can't find what you want there or in the index, you probably never will.

Keep training costs low. Look for tutorials, sample files, and plenty of worked through examples and illustrations to help you get started quickly and with confidence.

Your software dealer should sit down with you initially and show you and your personnel how to implement a software package. But as personnel come and go, or as you delegate data entry to subordinates, the manual will be your only instructor. Be sure it has a comprehensive reference section, an index, and a quick reference card.

Check With Other Users

One way to evaluate software would be to test it at your own installation. Of course, you cannot do this if you don't already own a computer. And few microcomputer software manufactures are willing to let you try their product on a trial basis. It is too easy to pirate material from one floppy disk to another.

Fortunately, or unfortunately, my staff has already suffered through a trial period with each of the packages reviewed in this book. (And many more we thought unsuitable for inclusion.) Still, our focus was that of a professional reviewer with our own needs and applications foremost in mind. Before you buy, check with other users, particularly those with similar applications. If your supplier will not give you names and telephone numbers of other users, look elsewhere for your software. Check with more than one user. Remember, what's good for one business may not be good for another.

Many users will try to put a bright face on a bad purchase. Listen for phrases like "I guess we didn't realize the computer's limitations," or "We only had to make a few alterations." Was it the computer's limitations or the software's? Were there many alterations? Custom programming can be very, very expensive and will mean delays in implementation.

A phrase I've learned to view with great suspicion is "We're grateful for all the help the store gave us." Help with what? Just how complicated is the software to use anyway? The software must stand on its own merits after an initial training period.

The Fine Points

Unfortunately, there are a number of fine points that you cannot get from a manual. One is speed-of-execution. A second is software compatibility.

We've eliminated from the comparison tables any software we felt was too slow for professional use. A full discussion of the limitations on software compatibility imposed by your computer and your computer's operating system is included in Chapter 14.

Some software is designed to stand alone and some to be integrated with other programs. There is merit in both approaches. Be on the lookout for software that will accept input or provide output to other programs that you may own or want to purchase later. WordStar, for example, is designed to work in harmony with all of MicroPro International's other software packages.

Ask About Safeguards

Two types of safeguards are emphasized in our reviews. The first protects against the accidental deletion of material, the second provides an opportunity for second thoughts. We've included both types in our comparison tables.

Safeguards are essential but not obvious features of software. They may not be listed in the manual and you may even overlook them when describing a program's features to someone else. Atari's word processor will let you *recall* the line you've just deleted in case you change your mind. Magic Wand will make you reenter a file name if there is a possibility of writing over an existing file.

Be safe. Buy software that has safeguards.

Make a Check List

Will your word processor meet *all* your needs? Some word processors can be used to create electronic mail, some Apple and Atari word processors cannot. A fine point, but one you can protect yourself against if you make a check list of your needs before you buy.

As you read each of the following chapters, make a list of the features that seem to meet specific or future needs. Your lists are your key to successful software selection.

CHECK LIST

A MASTER CHECK LIST
FOR SOFTWARE SELECTION

1-101. Know your application(s).

   • complete check list page 16.

102. Know what the software can do for you.

   • bare-bones features page 39.

   • text editor check list page 51.

   • printer formatter check list page 59.

   • extra features check list page 68.

103. Order the manual.

104. Check with current users.

105. Look for the fine points.

   • speed of execution.

   • compatibility with other applications software.

   • operating system limitations.

   • safeguards.

106. Make a check list.

CHAPTER 5

Bare-Bones Word Processing Software

A sophisticated word-processing system like those sold by CPT, Lanier or NBI can cost $15,000 and up. This may seem expensive but it is not if your application demands specialized features like Greek and Latin symbols, or the on-line display of chemical formula and mathematical expressions.

Not everyone needs to spend $15,000. The word processing needs of most small businesses can be met by a $5,000 to$ 7,000 desk-top computeand a $400 combined text editor, printer formatter and mail-merge program like Magic Wand or Spellbinder. And if your word processing needs are limited to electronic mail or post-ing the occasional notice on the CompuServe Bulletin Board, you can get the results you want with an Atari 400 ($325), a telephone modem ($149), and bare-bones word-processing software for only $19 more.

A bare-bones word processor will allow you to create and modify text files, display them on the screen, store and retrieve them, and produce a printed (hard) copy. Letter Writer for the Atari, for example, is $19 from CE Software. It has exactly five options: save a letter, load a letter, edit, print, and exit.

The *save/load* options are essential:

- You'll want to make minor modifications to the text.

- You'll want a copy on file to jog your memory or protect your legal interests.

- You'll want to use one letter as a template for others.

Most business correspondence consists of three or four standard letters with minor modifications to fit the situation. With the aid of a word processor, even the bare-bones version, you can load an existing document or letter, make the necessary modifications, and save the revised document under a different name.

The *edit* option of the Letter Writer makes use of the Atari's built-in editing features. In fact, the Letter Writer only supplies two editing features of its own. You use the Atari insert key to insert text, and the Atari delete key to delete text errors. Letter Writer provides two additional commands that let you indent paragraphs and skip lines.

There are many things you can't do with Letter Writer that you can do with more expensive word-processing software. For example, you can't make the computer scan the text to look for a particular word or phrase, which could be essential if you are indexing or making repeated changes throughout a long document.

The Letter Writer *print* option allows you to set the line length (though not the left margin), insert new pages as required, and right justify your text just like a book or magazine. You can use this inexpensive bare-bones word-processor to make good use of an expensive letter-quality printer.

Less Can Mean More

The **Mini-processor** for the Atari is just $15 from Santa Cruz Educational Software. It costs less than the Letter Writer, but it has a few more editing features.

The Mini-processor allows you to create files, save or load them, modify them, and create hard copy. While editing, you have full control over the Atari's tab, delete, back space, clear, insert, and cursor control keys. But you can also advance through the text a page at a time or move with a single command to the beginning or end of the text. You may interchange pages of text, though you cannot cut and paste any section smaller than a page.

The Mini-processor works with either parallel or serial printers, using an Atari 850 interface.

For the Apple and the Model III

Not surprisingly, one of the best bare-bones word proces-sors for the Apple was designed by a company that spe-cializes in telecommunications. It's the **Correspondent** for $35 from Southwestern Data Systems. The Correspondent costs more, but in addition to the basics it provides for locating a word or phrase anywhere in the text, and for moving, copying or deleting blocks of text of any size, its manual includes a ten-page section of practice exercises.

DART for the Apple, $20 from Service Unique, provides an additional feature, the entry of variable text into a report. You'll find this feature essential for mass mailings. Each time the processor encounters a variable word or name in the text, it stops so that you can supply the *personalized* information from the keyboard.

Kwikwrite for the TRS-80 Model III costs $38 from M. B. Rowe & Associates. Kwikwrite actually incorporates four different programs, each of which is "pre-formatted" for a specific task such as creating a cover page, a label, or the first page of a standard letter. While Kwikwrite does more for you if your application fits its intentions, its lack of flexibility may drive you berserk. For example, you've got to create a different file for each page of your text.

The Letter-Writer for the Radio Shack Model I or Model III, $39 from Astro-Star Enterprises, is a far better buy. It even includes a built-in calculator for simple accounting.

Preparing Electronic Mail

You can use a bare-bones processor to create notes and text for electronic bulletin boards or to draft electronic mail. Your line costs and connect time charges won't begin until you are through editing. You'll save money and you won't tie up your telephone lines.

Surprisingly, you can't prepare files off-line for transmission with one of the more expensive word processors for the Atari—LJK's Letter Perfect ($140). You can modify text files off-line but not on-line with a second, Data Soft's TextWizard ($99).

The developers of the more expensive Letter Perfect and Text Wizard are quite concerned about software piracy. They chose to sacrifice user convenience in favor of methods that prevent illegal copying.

Letter Perfect stores its files in a special format that can be read only by the Letter Perfect software. You won't be able to transmit those files over telephone lines except as binary files, and you can't post binary files on an electronic bulletin board. Despite its price, Letter Perfect can't be used for electronic mail.

You can transmit messages prepared with Text Wizard, but you can't modify them while you're still on the telephone. That's because the Text Wizard program itself is protected. I've solved the problem by using not one but two word processors. I use Text Wizard to create my letters—it has many more editing features than a bare-bones word processor—and I use Letter-Writer if I need to make one or two changes while I'm on the telephone.

Moving Up to Schlitz

There comes a time when you decide you want more than a bare-bones word processor. You want a global search and replace feature. You want to dress up your output with single and double spacing, underlining, and **bold face**.

Before you spend $140 for a more expensive word processor like Letter-Perfect, or $445 for MicroPro's **WordStar**, consider investing in a line-by-line editor like Interactive Microware's **Pro-Type**, $99 for the North Star Horizon. Line-by-line editors cost only one-half as much as their full-screen counterparts. They have many, many desirable features including deleting or inserting entire blocks of text, and global search and replace. But they are limited to editing one line at a time.

If your chief interest is in creating and editing computer programs, a line editor may be a best buy. Even then, it can be worth paying extra for the convenience of a full screen text editor like Vedit ($145) that can be tailored for the programmer. A line editor is a good choice for electronic mail. But so is the Mini-processor, and it provides a full-screen editor at a cost of only $15.

In almost every application, you will find that the convenience of a full-screen editor will more than justify the additional cost (if any). Don't just move up to Schlitz, move up to Lowenbrau.

CHECK LIST

BARE-BONES WORD PROCESSOR FEATURES

1. File Control

   • Save, load, update

   • Display file directory

2. Edit

   • Delete, insert lines and characters

   • Jump through text

   • Move, copy, or delete blocks

   • Search for phrases

3. Prepare files for transmission

4. Print

   • Set line length

   • Justify margins

   • Work with several printer types

   • Merge files with keyboard entries

   • Special formats for letters and labels

CHECK LIST

VENDORS LIST OF BARE-BONES WORD PROCESSORS

Letter Writer CE Software 238 Exchange St. Chicopee, MA 01013 (413) 592-4761	$19	Atari
Mini-processor Santa Cruz Educational Software 5425 Jigger Dr. Soquel, CA 95073 (408)476-4901	$15	Atari
Correspondent Southwestern Data Systems 10159-G Mission Gorge Rd. Santee, CA 92071 (714) 562-3670	$35	Apple
DART Service Unique 2441 Rolling View Dr. Dayton, OH 45431	$20	Apple
Kwikwrite M.B. Rowe Associates PO Box 1192 Hickory, NC 28603	$38	TRS-80 111

Letter-Writer	$39	TRS-80 111
Astro-Star Enterprises		
5905 Stone Hill Dr.		
Rocklin, CA 95677		
(916) 624-3709		

C.C. Writer	$35	TRS Color
Transformation Technologies		Computer
194 Lockwood Lane		
Bloomingdale, IL 60108		

CHAPTER 6

Selecting
A
Text Editor

Word processing requires two programs: a text editor which will help you to *edit* the text of a manuscript or a computer program, and a printer formatter which *formats* the text so that it can be printed according to your specifications. Most word processors incorporate both programs, though you can purchase an editor and a formatter separately.

A text editor can help you to create errorless manuscripts, expedite your correspondence, and speed up program development. The purpose of this chapter is to review some of the functions that are common to all text editors, to show you how these functions can be applied in your own work, and to provide you with criteria for selecting a text editor.

The basic text editing functions may be grouped under four headings: edits, *moves, searches,* and *document control.*

Edits—The full-screen editor provides you with an electronic tablet. You leaf through the pages by a series of commands, and move your place marker (a cursor) as freely as a pencil to any phrase that needs modification. You can insert or delete a symbol, a word, or a paragraph. You won't need an eraser and you won't need to retype a thrice-corrected document. Your hand-corrected copy will always be as neat as the original.

Drawing courtesy of Perfect Software

An imaginative drawing to illustrate
scrolling process

Moves—A logical extension of the full-screen edit is the ability to insert text of any length at any point in a document and to shift material (cut and paste) from one place to another within the text. Peach Text, for example, provides for block insert, block move, block copy and block delete of any portion of a document that is currently held in memory.

Searches—A search facility makes it easy for you to resume editing at any point in the text by asking the computer to look for a given word or phrase. You might ask for the section headed *Searches* or any phrase that begins *Sea*. Some editors allow you to use wild cards; *Se...es* is all you need to ask. old The ideal text editor will have the ability to do a global search and replace; that is, it will look for and replace *old* with *new* at every point *old* appears in the document by using just one command.

Documents—Document control is the guts of any data processing system. You'll be saving letters and manuscripts as documents on floppy disks. You'll want to backup documents while editing, insert one document within another, display a directory of documents, and erase existing documents to create more room for new ones. A document control feature that makes the Peach Text word processor particularly attractive is the ability to work with up to five documents simultaneously: reading from one, inserting a second, spooling a third to the printer, displaying a fourth, and writing the results to a fifth.

Hidden Factors

Although almost all desk-top word processors provide these features, the ability to make them work for you will vary widely from text editor to text editor and from computer to computer. Style, flexibility, safeguards, and speed of execution will be the chief factors that influence your final choice.

Two principal styles

Some editors assign an editing command to almost every character on the keyboard. The command function is implemented by depressing the *ctrl* or *esc* key simultaneously along with the character. (See drawing on opposite page.) Others use just a few keys, typically the numeric key pad, over and over, although the meaning assigned to a given key will change with the context.

With some editors, as you add new text it will push the old text ahead of it. If you want to eliminate the old text, an additional delete operation is required. With other editors, you can correct a misspelled word just by typing the new word over the old. But you need to use a special command to insert a new word without erasing the old one. One word processor, Perfect Writer, will give you a choice between the two methods.

I still prefer the latter, though that may be from force of habit. I have more definite prejudices regarding two styles of movement through the text. I call the styles DEC and IBM respectively, after their mainframe computer originals. The two styles differ in how you view the text, in the way characters are inserted and deleted, and in how the editing operations are controlled. If you aren't a DEC programmer by profession, you will probably prefer the IBM style, with some exceptions I've noted below.

The DEC style limits the cursor to horizontal movement. Vertical movement is accomplished by scrolling the text itself up and down the screen. If you try to use the

CURSOR Command Summary:

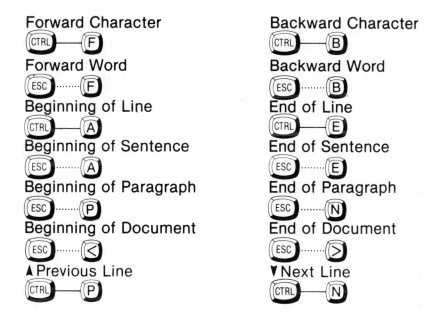

Forward Character
CTRL — F

Forward Word
ESC ...... F

Beginning of Line
CTRL — A

Beginning of Sentence
ESC ...... A

Beginning of Paragraph
ESC ...... P

Beginning of Document
ESC ...... <

▲ Previous Line
CTRL — P

Backward Character
CTRL — B

Backward Word
ESC ...... B

End of Line
CTRL — E

End of Sentence
ESC ...... E

End of Paragraph
ESC ...... N

End of Document
ESC ...... >

▼ Next Line
CTRL — N

SCREEN Command Summary:

View Previous Screen
CTRL — Z

Exchange Cursor and Mark
CTRL — X   CTRL — X

View Next Screen
CTRL — V

Drawing courtesy of Perfect Software

An example of how some text editors assign an editing command to almost every character on the Keyboard. To activate the command, the ctrl or esc key is depressed simultaneously along with the character.

cursor control keys for vertical movement, the cursor may jump to the end of a sentence or the entire display may scroll forward instead. I find the entire effect disconcerting.

The one advantage is that the text on which you are working tends to be centered on the screen, with the surrounding text immediately visible above and below. It's the style used by Perfect Writer, Spellbinder, and Vedit. But unless you are an experienced DEC programmer, I think you will prefer the style used by Peach Text and WordStar in which you have full control over the cursor.

Style and Flexibility

In any event, I've found that style is far less important than flexibility–the ability to adapt to the needs of a given application.

For example, Peach Text offers four types of text insert: typeover, push ahead, insert mode, and block. Typeover is pure IBM style–you insert text by typing over (and thus replacing) the old text. Push ahead mode is pure DEC style–you can add text almost as fast as you type, providing you don't push ahead too far. It is the ideal way to enter the occasional apostrophe or extra "s" that you neglected to type on the first writing.

You may insert an unlimited amount of text in insert mode. But you can not see the text that follows while you are inserting the new material. Slight pauses as you enter and exit make Spellbinder's insert mode wasteful of time for adding a single word or character, but appropriate for adding a sentence or a paragraph. The block mode of insert is used when you want to move or copy material from some other part of the text. I would not like to do without any of these methods of data entry, as I have applications which require them all.

Too Much Flexibility

On the other hand, there can be too much flexibility. The Spellbinder word processing package provides for switching between 'character,' 'word,' 'sentence,' and 'paragraph' modes. I found the flexibility dangerous. Intending to delete a word, I deleted an entire paragraph.

Both Spellbinder and Peach Text do offer safeguards against deleting large amounts of material but only if the block mode of delete is used. Spellbinder asks "really?" giving you a chance to think it over if more than 1024 characters of text are involved. You must reply "Y" for yes to confirm the delete. Peach Text asks for confirmation regarding a block delete of text of any length. Peach Text also cautions you if you attempt to delete a document, whether you do it deliberately or inadvertently by assigning the name of an existing document to a second unrelated document.

The value of any and all safeguards cannot be underestimated. It's to the lasting discredit of both manufacturers and distributors that too few manuals and sales presentations mention safeguards, even when they exist. Once you've narrowed your choice of text editors, see a demonstration if possible. Then, ask to see the safeguards demonstrated.

Speed of Execution

All the word processors listed in the tables at the end of this book have met minimal standards for speed-of-execution. One text editor that did not is Copywriter, distributed by Systronics Business Systems, Hasbrouck Heights NJ. Copywriter is a big program, not all of which is stored in memory at one time. Copywriter constantly needs to access the disk drives. Each access is two orders of magnitude slower than a transaction that takes place entirely within the computer's memory.

You can't realize the extent of such delays, and the irritation occasioned by them, without trying out a word processor for yourself. Consider the difference in the way you would use two text editors, Peach Text and Copywriter, to delete the extra "e" from "Deelete":

With Peach Text, you would begin by positioning the cursor on the letter "e"; then you would hold down the control key and type "d". The operation is complete. With Copywriter, you also begin by positioning the cursor and typing a "d". Copywriter would pause to access the disk in order to enter its 'delete' mode. When the keyboard was again enabled, you would type a space over the extra "e", followed by a "Q" to quit. Copywriter would access the disk again before returning to the edit mode. The text would reappear, and, as with Peach Text, "Delete" would be spelled correctly. Your irritation would be severe, however.

Two Quick Tests

If you have the opportunity for a hands-on demonstration, here are two quick tests of a text editor's efficiency: First, count the number of operations needed to delete a single letter or punctuation mark. This is an important test, as you will need to delete a single letter (usually a misspelling) about ten times as often as any other editing operation. Second, do a global search and replace. The word 'the' occurs with a very high frequency in most text. Ask the word processor to replace 'the' with 'test' every place 'the' occurs in a text. Peach Text can do a global search and replace a five page document in less than three seconds.

CHECK LIST
TEXT EDITOR FEATURES

Check if desired
or essential

FILE CONTROL

_____ continuous back-up
_____ save file and continue editing
_____ automatic back-up on file save
_____ file protect safeguard
_____ insert a second file with one command
_____ insert a portion of a second file
_____ display a second file
_____ display file directory
_____ file (and create space)
_____ prepare files for transmission

EDITS

1 SCROLLING (or cursor movement)

_____ by word
_____ by line or by sentence
_____ by screen or by page
_____ to beginning or end
_____ horizontal scroll

2 DELETE

_____ by character
_____ by word
_____ by line
_____ by sentence
_____ by screen
_____ continuous delete

3 INSERT

_____ key phrases

———— typeover (fast)
———— insert mode (for many words)
———— push ahead (for one or two letters)
———— split and glue a line at a time
———— intermediate buffer

BLOCKS EDITS

———— block delete
———— block delete safeguard
———— block move
———— block copy

SEARCH

———— find phrase
———— find with user option to replace
———— find and replace n times
———— find and replace all
———— use wild cards
———— ignore upper/lower case in matching

CHAPTER 7

Basics of
a Good
Printer Formatter

One measure of the youth of the desk-top computer industry is the casual freedom with which its practitioners brand their wares. Thus we have "Michael Shrayer's Electric Pencil," "Bob's Mini-Processor," and the classic "Scribble" from a company called "Mark of the Unicorn." The first of the printer formatters, **Textwriter**, was developed by "Organic Software," a company located in the heart of the natural foods' belt of Northern California.

You will enhance the appearance of your programs and reports with the aid of a printer formatter. A good formatter provides you with maximum control over the form of your printed output while minimizing the need for your intervention. Most word processors include a printer formatter as well as a text editor. "Textwriter" by contrast was designed for the programmer or software developer who is making do with the text editor that comes with his computer. But it illustrates many of the capabilities of the best printer formatters that are available today.

Textwriter provides for laying out text on the printed page including top, bottom, left and right margins where any and all of these may be different from the way the text appears on the screen. Its commands are embedded within the text of the manuscript, so that the layout may be altered from page to page or paragraph to paragraph as you choose.

Textwriter will overrule preset formats to avoid leaving an isolated word or line at the bottom of a page, or splitting tables. You can call for automatic page numbering, and specify multiline headings and footings which may be different for odd or even, right facing or left facing pages. Space is automatically reserved for footnotes.

More Features

Printer formatters also provide for justifying text, (padding a line with blanks or spaces between the letters so that the margins come out even like those of a magazine), centering titles, and hyphenating words at the end of lines.

Hyphenation can never be completely automatic, as there are too many rules for even a sophisticated computer to remember. But many printer formatters allow you to insert a "phantom" or soft hyphen within a word. If the word occurs in the middle of the line, the soft hyphen is ignored. If the word won't fit at the end of the line, the computer breaks it at the soft hyphen.

The text of this book has been embellished with **BOLD** titles, and <u>underlined material</u> under the direction of a printer formatter.

There are no formulas in this book, so we didn't use a superscript or a subscript. Nor did we change ribbon colors. You'll need a printer formatter to help you to do all these things, and to take advantage of any special features of the newer models of dot-matrix printers like expanded or condensed text.

Extended Features

Those formatters which go beyond the basics, do so in one of two ways: by letting you preview the text on the screen as it will appear in print, and by permitting greater flexibility in the time and manner in which formatting commands are issued.

PeachText lets you alter the line length as you edit. The results can be quite deceptive as control characters are not excluded, and words are not hyphenated, as they would be on the printed page. With Benchmark, on the other hand, what you see is what you get.

SuperScribe II lets you embed format commands in the text while editing, and/or set them from a menu, and/or issue new instructions while printing. SuperScreen II lets you make two passes through a text, printing only certain materials on each pass, using a different type face each time.

Making Correspondence Easy

One of the most desirable extended features is the ability to create a form letter, one that can be personalized with each printing. On the next page is a form letter template I used to request copies of the word-processing software reviewed for this book.

At line 1, embedded format commands determine the left, right, top and bottom margins of the letter. At line 2, the computer pauses to ask me for the date. At line 3, I am asked to provide the information—name, company, street, city and zip code—needed to create an inside address.

At line 4, the computer begins printing the letter. Each time the printer formatter encounters a variable name in the text like :COMPANY or :TITLE, it prints the name of the company or the title of the program that was just entered.

The letter has different strokes for different folks. If I want the CP/M version of a program, I enter an M to trigger the printing of the appropriate request at line 5. I have the computer pause at line 6 so that I may enter a 'personalized' postscript from the keyboard. Judging by the quantity of software I obtained for review, such 'personalized' form letters can be very effective.

CHECK LIST

TEMPLATE
FOR A FORM LETTER

1. %LM12, RM55, TM13, BM6, FORMS

2. %:Date%

3. %:NAME%

    %:COMPANY%

    %:ADDR1%

    %:ADDR2%

4. Dear %:Name%:

    I would like to receive a copy of your program %:TITLE% for review in my book "Choosing a Desktop Word Processor", and in our newsletters *The Office Automation Letter* and the *Laboratory Computer Letter.*

    Here are the materials I will need for review purposes:

    • all manuals

    and,

5. %if MACH = "A"

    • a disk that will run on the Apple II Plus %if MACH = "I"

• a disk that will run on the Atari 800
%if MACH = "M"

• an 8 inch single density disk, CP/M 2.2

For additional information, please call me at (891)

688-2159. If you would like to verify my status, please

consult current issues of Computer Dealer, Computer

Decisions, Computer Shopper, or Popular Computing.

Very truly yours,

%Insert 3 lines

Phillip Good, Ph.D.

6. %Insert personalized postscript

CHECK LIST

PRINTER FORMATTER FEATURES

Check if desired
or essential

LAYOUT

_____ set from a menu
_____ menu may be skipped
_____ under user control while printing
_____ characters per inch
_____ lines per inch

PAGE CONTROL

_____ one line heading
_____ multi-line heading
_____ heading and footing
_____ page numbering
_____ odd/even page distinction
_____ discretionary new page

TEXT CONTROL

_____ justify
_____ center
_____ phantom hyphen
_____ multiply columns
_____ reverse line feed

PRINTER CONTROL

_____ underline
_____ bold face
_____ vary bold face intensity
_____ super- and sub-script

———— change ribbon colors
———— kerning
———— change control characters
———— proportional spacing

OUTPUT CONTROL

———— interrupt, resume
———— alter format
———— pause for text entry from keyboard
———— pause for variable entry
———— print multiple copies
———— display on screen as it will print
———— mail-merge or file-merge

CHAPTER 8

Some
Extra Features

Readers have asked me one question more frequently than any other in the two years I've been contributing columns to computer and office magazines: "Should we buy WordStar or Magic Wand for our office?" I mail out a standard answer: "Your choice of word processor will depend on your application." But occasionally, when I think of menus, I'm tempted to expose my true gut feeling: "Forget them both."

Menus

WordStar has lots of menus. Now, menus are great sales aids in showrooms. They give the impression that the computer is really doing the job by itself, requiring only

An example of a typical word processing menu. A few menus are desirable.

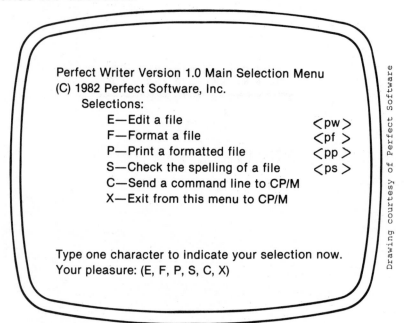

Perfect Writer Version 1.0 Main Selection Menu
(C) 1982 Perfect Software, Inc.
    Selections:
        E—Edit a file   \<pw\>
        F—Format a file   \<pf \>
        P—Print a formatted file   \<pp \>
        S—Check the spelling of a file \<ps \>
        C—Send a command line to CP/M
        X—Exit from this menu to CP/M

Type one character to indicate your selection now.
Your pleasure: (E, F, P, S, C, X)

Drawing courtesy of Perfect Software

the occasional intervention of some low form of human life. Menus are a valuable aid during installation or the initial set up of a complex page format. But they are a nuisance when they must be consulted routinely, or when, as with the DEC and WordStar word processing systems, they are encountered one after another in a seemingly endless procession.

Help commands and help panels on the other hand, particularly those that remain hidden until you want them, are indispensable. Select reserves several lines at the top of the screen to display its editing commands. A menu is also provided for setting page formats. Spellbinder also provides a menu for setting page formats; unfortunately, you have to have the manual in your hand to figure out how to use it.

Spellbinder has one other unusual menu feature. Two versions of the program are supplied. One, for beginners, uses half of the screen for a display of the commands. The second, for experienced users, frees the full screen for editing.

Magic Wand (now sold under the name Peach Text) has no menus. A help panel is provided during printing, not editing, as an aid to modifying page formats. There is a help command (which you won't find listed in the manual) that will provide a cryptic listing of the possible file commands. That's it. You're on your own, apart from a detachable command reference card that can be propped up by the terminal.

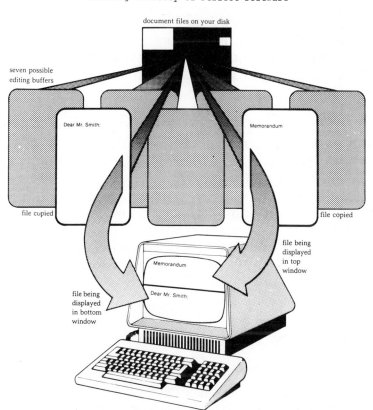

Drawing courtesy of Perfect Software

Console screen provides a separate window on two different documents.

Editing Large Documents

Many of the editing features described in Chapter 6 will not work if the document is too large to fit into memory as a single block. Features such as scroll forward, or search and replace, will apply only to the portion of the document that is actually in memory. These restrictions will affect only documents with twenty or more pages, for the most part. If your computer's memory has 32K or less, almost every document will be adversely affected.

If you work frequently with large documents, you want a word processor that is capable of working with documents in sections, writing from memory to disk and reading from disk to memory as each section is completed. With Magic Wand, the procedure is only semiautomatic; the user has to initiate each read/write sequence. With WordStar, the replacement takes place without user intervention.

WordStar offers other important advantages. Scrolling, paging, search and replace commands apply to the entire document, not just the section that is in memory. Even with WordStar, significant delays are occasioned by each disk access. If you routinely work with large documents— books or lengthy reports—consider purchasing a hard disk drive to reduce the length of such delays. The trade off against the cost of the drive (the least expensive is about $5,000) is the cost of your time and your staff's time.

Programmers' Requirements

Programmers have special requirements. Here are three examples. First, all carriage returns must be eliminated. The ubiquitous carriage return which marks the end of each line of a document cannot be permitted within the text of a program for fear it will be misinterpreted by the computer executing the program. Second, each line of a Basic program must be numbered. Third, good programming practice, whether in Basic, Pascal or PL/I, requires that each line be indented. Not all word processors are capable of meeting these three requirements. But many do offer carriage return suppression, automatic line numbering (useful too for legal documents), and multiple tabs and indents.

One other "extra" feature, borrowed from mainframe word processors, has proved particularly attractive to programmers—multiple file or split screen displays. The split-screen feature is invaluable to anyone whose work builds on previous efforts: to a programmer who reuses code from an earlier program; to an attorney who reuses clauses from previous contracts. It is easy to interchange whole sections and paragraphs, when the old and the new file can be viewed simultaneously.

Mail-Merge

I often use a word processor to create form-letters. In the example given in Chapter 7, the inside address was entered from the keyboard. There are two drawbacks to this method of entry. First, I must type the address all over again on the envelope; second, I have no record of my addressees. With a *mail-merge* option, I enter the inside address and other variable information into a separate file. I do this once and once only. When I go to print my letters, the word processor merges the two files containing the letter and the addresses. I reuse the address file to create labels for the envelopes, and, if I wish to send out follow-up letters in the succeeding months, I can reuse the file again and again.

Some word processors supplement their mail-merge programs with features usually associated with far more expensive data base management systems. As an example, Spellbinder provides routines to sort the address file by zip code or by first or last name. (The last is a bit tricky if you think about it. In a name like Bill Smith, Jr, somehow the computer must skip over Bill and then ignore the Jr to 'decide' that S is the first letter of the last name. Spellbinder succeeds with this sort feature.)

Getting More From Your Equipment

No matter how infrequently you use your computer, there comes a day when you wish you had two of everything. Perhaps you have to prepare a financial report, revise it, and mail it to a stack of addresses all in one day. The problem could be resolved quickly if you could just work on the report while your secretary printed the address file. But when she's on the terminal, you're not, and visa versa. The amount of equipment that was right for the average day-to-day effort collapses in the crunch.

A partial solution is available *if* you have the right software, and the right dealer support. The technical term is spooling; the practical implication is that you are able to use your printer and your video terminal simultaneously and independently for different tasks. But you'll need help to do it.

Magic Wand is one of the few word processors that can be modified to let you print one document while editing another. But the makers of Magic Wand won't make the modifications for you. That's because those modifications require access to and understanding of the documentation for your particular model of computer, and there are just too many models for Magic Wand's makers to keep track of. The manufacturer of your computer won't make the modifications either. That's because the modifications re-quire a detailed knowledge of the Magic Wand software. If you order Magic Wand or any other word processor with spooling capability, insist that the spooling capability be installed by your dealer before you make payment.

Spelling Checkers

One other worthwhile extra feature is the spelling checker, which can cost between $75 and $195 if purchased separately. The money stays in your pocket if a spelling checker is included in the price of the word processing software as it is with Select. But is that spelling checker the best one for you? Spelling checkers and their features are reviewed in the next chapter.

CHECK LIST
EXTRA FEATURES

Check if desired
or essential

1. Menus
_____ available
_____ may be suppressed or by-passed
_____ help files available

2. Large documents
_____ processes documents larger than memory
_____ processes large documents without interventio
_____ search and replace not limited to memory

3. Multiple files
_____ display a second file
_____ display two files simultaneously
_____ print one file while editing a second

4. Mail-merge
_____ addresses may be entered from keyboard
_____ addresses may be entered from files
_____ can sort addresses by zip code or name

5. Spelling Checker
   Dictionary
_____ size (20,000-40,000 words)
_____ compactness (less than   bytes)
_____ accuracy
_____ ease of adding new words
_____ ease of deleting bad entries

Ease of use
_____ displays repeated errors once only
_____ displays errors in context on request
_____ displays hyphenated words
_____ suggests correct spelling
_____ inserts corrections in text

_____ 6. Format options

_____ 7. Help files available on-line

CHAPTER 9

Spelling Checkers

You *luse* credibility if you don't spell correctly. No matter how poor a speller we may be ourselves, we still judge others by their spelling. We can forgive slips of the tongue in face-to-face contact, but once it's on paper we become stern critics. Unfortunately, that cuts both ways. When we put our own thoughts on paper, we'll be judged by the results, not the intentions.

Looking for spelling errors is time-consuming. But it's precisely such unglamorous time-consuming drudgery that computers were designed to handle. We think you'll find a *spelling checker* to be essential.

MicroProof, which was used to correct this book, has

a 40,000 word dictionary. It can scan a 10 page document in 100 seconds. It displays every word not found in its dictionary so that you can mark the word as incorrect, or add the word to its dictionary. If you ask, it will display the word in context so you can recall whether 'broon' was intended to be 'broom' or 'brown' or something else entirely. Finally, MicroProof will substitute the correct spellings in the text and update its dictionary, both automatically.

Proofing a document

When you or I check a document for misspellings, we proceed a word at a time, referring to the dictionary as needed, making corrections as we go. This is the method employed by the IBM Displaywriter. While this method may seem intuitive and natural in a person, it's incredibly wasteful both of machine time and personnel when employed by a computer. It's more efficient for a computer to proceed in stages: first, proof the document, checking for errors; second, review the error list, allowing a person to overrule your machine judgment; and finally, make the necessary corrections to the original document.

We examined the same 2000 word document with The Word, SpellGuard, WordSearch, MicroProof and IBM's Displaywriter. WordSearch and the Displaywriter took 3 minutes, MicroProof and The Word each took 1 minute and 10 seconds, and SpellGuard took only 40 seconds. However, SpellGuard left us with 12 more words to review than The Word did.

Dictionary Size

A spelling checker proofs a document by checking each word against a list of words that are in its "dictionary." If its dictionary is a small one, it may conclude that almost every word in your document is "misspelled," leaving you with as much work to do in straightening out the mess as if you had proofed the document by hand in the first place.

How big a dictionary is big enough? Do you really need a 50,000 word dictionary? I don't think so. Too large a dictionary can slow things down, particularly if the dictionary, like that of MicroSpell, requires more than one disk.

Twenty thousand words is about right. Almost all the spelling checkers I reviewed will give you the opportunity to add words to the dictionary. After five months of using SpellGuard to check my columns, I'd added exactly 543 words—mainly on computer topics. A head to head comparison of my enhanced SpellGuard dictionary (20,543 words) with the original dictionary supplied by The Word (45,000 words), left SpellGuard with only 6 more words set aside for review (three of them with hyphens), and a clear time advantage.

SpellGuard didn't recognize 'saucer' and 'Montreal'. It also didn't recognize "anti-climactic" and "he'd", two words that The Word accepted because The Word has been programmed to watch out for hyphens and apostrophes. Don't be deceived; this comparison favors SpellGuard since 'anticlimactic' is not supposed to be hyphenated.

IBM's Displaywriter has a 45,000 word dictionary. But you can't add words to it during the review phase. You have to re-enter (and retype) them at a later time, and even then they can only be entered in blocks of 500 words. You almost need a second spelling checker along with the Displaywriter to help you build a technical dictionary.

In fairness to the Displaywriter, it does permit the user to check spelling in context. Only two of the desk-top spelling checkers, MicroProof from Cornucopia Software and MicroSpell from Lifeboat Associates, offer a similar feature.

MicroProof and MicroSpell both insert your corrections in the text, automatically. Beware of spelling checkers that just do part of the job. They flag the errors in the text, but leave it to you to make the corrections. That can be time consuming.

In summary, look for features in a spelling checker that can save you time:

• single pass error checking

• large enough dictionary—at least 20,000 words

• display words in context

• suggest the "correct" spelling

• insert corrections in the text

Now for the bad news

Of course, this summary assumes that the words in the dictionary are spelled correctly. If a word is misspelled in the dictionary, a spelling checker will overlook a similar misspelling in a document. We took a quick pass by eye through WordSearch's dictionary one day and found twenty spelling errors in a few minutes. An exhaustive search of SpellGuard's dictionary yielded just 15 misspellings, all but 2 of which have been corrected in the latest revision.

CHECK LIST

VENDORS LIST OF SPELLING CHECKERS

Chextext
Apparat Inc.
4401 S. Tamarac Blvd
Denver CO 80237
TRS-80 Model III
10,000 words

Dic-tio-nary
On-Line Systems
36575 Mudge Ranch Rd
Coarsegold CA 93614
(209) 683-6858
Apple II
28,000 words

Electric Webster
Cornucopia Software
PO Box 5028
Walnut Creek CA 94596
(415) 893-0633
For CP/M based computers or all models of TRS-80. 50,000 word dictionary Suggests correct spelling

Hexspell
Hexspell Systems
Box 397
Vancouver BC V6C2N2
TRS-80 Model III
10,000 word dictionary is too small

Magic Spell
Artsi Inc.
10432 Burbank Blv'd
North Hollywood CA 91601
(213) 985-2922
Apple II
14,000 words
Doesn't correct errors

75

Product	Company / Address	Description
MicroProof (Blue Pencil)	Cornucopia Software PO Box 5028 Walnut Creek CA 94596 (415) 893-0633	For CP/M based computers or all models of TRS-80. 25,000 word dictionary Corrects errors in context
MicroSpell	Lifeboat Associates 1651 Third Ave New York NY 10028 (212) 860-0300	For CP/M based computers 25,000 word dictionary Will 'suggest' correct spelling Difficulties with large documents
MIZ Spell	Programs Unlimited Box 265 Jericho, NY 11753	TRS-80 Model I 18,000 words
Proofreader	Aspen Software MHE Box 14 Tijeras NM 87059	TRS-80 Model III 38,000 words Doesn't correct errors
Sensible Speller	Sensible Software 6619 Perham Dr W. Bloomfield MI 48033 (313) 399-8877	Apple, Apple with CP/M 30,000 word dictionary
Spell (Perfect Spell)	Software Toolworks 14478 Glorietta Dr Sherman Oaks CA 91423 (213) 986-4885	A dictionary to fit any CP/M system; flexible. Doesn't correct errors

Spell Star	Micro Pro International 1299 4th St San Rafael CA 94901 (415) 457-8990	To be used with WordStar on CP/M based computers 20,000 word dictionary
SpellGuard (Peach Spell Superspell)	Sorcim, Inc 915 Timothy Lane Menlo Park CA 94025 (415) 326-0805	CP/M based computers 20,000 word dictionary Doesn't correct errors
The Word Plus (crossword)	Oasis Systems 2765 Reynard Way San Diego CA 92103 (714) 291-9489	CP/M based computers 45,000 word dictionary Suggests correct spelling
Wordcheck	MicroComputer Industries 1520 E Mulberry Fort Collins CO 80524 (303) 221-1955	To be used with WordPro on the Pet. 9,000 word dictionary
WordSearch	Key Bits Inc 15425 SW 88th Ave Miami FL 33159 (305) 238 3820	CP/M based computers 10,000 word dictionary Lots of bugs in our copy

PART 3
HARDWARE

CHAPTER 10

Components of
a Desktop
Computer System

Remember when you got your first stereo? You played every record three times and you turned the bass way up. Then you got to college and your roommate had components. He had an amplifier and a pre-amp, a trail of wires that went around the room, and a huge pair of speakers that constantly brought the dorm resident to your door.

Buying a computer for word processing can be like that—you can buy an off-the-shelf model that includes almost everything built-in, or you can buy components. Not only will the computer components be of higher quality but they will be less expensive! The purpose of this chapter is to tell you what components you'll need, what desirable properties to look for in each one, and even a couple of brand names to get you started. But remember, buying a small computer is no different than buying a large one: to get the right computer you have to know your application.

The first and hardest lesson is that the actual computer is the least expensive part of a computer system.

You may have seen advertisements—a computer for $500 or even $399. The fact is they could give computers away and you would still spend five to six thousand dollars before you left the store.

A complete desktop system consists of the following:

• An input device like a typewriter keyboard for entering information.

• Output devices like a video screen or cathode ray tube (CRT) for displaying information and a printer for producing hard copy.

• A central processing unit (the computer) containing a computer-on-a-chip, read only memory (ROM) and random access memory (RAM).

• The interconnections and interfaces between the components. More than mere wires, these interfaces can be micro-computers themselves; they are expensive and are seldom included in the basic system price.

• Mass storage devices like a floppy disk drive or a cassette recorder for storing large quantities of information—data bases or quarterly reports— outside the computer's main memory.

All the above components are referred to collectively as the hardware. Obviously, the system is still incomplete

CHECK LIST

COMPONENTS OF
A DESKTOP WORD PROCESSOR

1. Applications Software

2. Input Device or Terminal

3. Output Device or Printer

4. The Computer

    i   computer-on-a-chip

    ii direct access memory

    iii buses and interfaces

5. Mass Storage Devices

    floppy disk drives

6. The Operating System

CHAPTER 11

Choosing a Terminal

Although there are cases on record where computers have fallen into disuse, usually, when the computer was bought on impulse, without regard to its future applications, in the vast majority of cases, use of your computer terminal soon will rise to eight or more hours a day. All the factors involved in choosing a terminal are variations on a single theme—comfort.

The Keyboard

A video terminal consists of two parts, a keyboard and a television screen, though they may be housed in a single unit. The keyboard should resemble one with which you and your staff are already familiar. With the variety of keyboards available today, there is no reason why the location and shape of its keys should not be identical to a keyboard you already own and have mastered.

Obviously, you'll want to take a test spin of an hour or two on a terminal before you buy. *Have the employee who will use the terminal test the terminal.* Put your hands on the keyboard; your fingers should automatically land upon the right keys. If not, forget that terminal. If there is any question in your mind, use a ruler or a pair of calipers to check the spacing. Nothing can be as frustrating as a keyboard that isn't quite right.

In the early days of desk-top computers, a few were made with keys that weren't separated, that didn't depress, that didn't click, and that didn't push back. These were in-human keyboards, marvels of technology, and a constant source of irritation to the hardy few who did attempt their use. There were exceptions—the Apple has prospered despite its lack of an upper/lower case shift key, and the bizarre keyboard locations of some characters like the quotes symbol.

Check the Spacing

The spacing on the Apple's keyboard feels correct to the hand. By contrast, the Atari 800 has its right shift key exactly one half inch to the right of where it should be. The Atari's quote symbol, which is used repeatedly when programming in Atari Basic, is located above the two (2) key, rather than to the right of the colon (:) where it belongs.

Designers of terminal keyboards have had to resolve a number of challenges not present in the more pedestrian typewriter. They've had to find 'human' locations for the 'extra' keys that control specific computer functions. These include cursor control keys, a numeric key pad, special function keys, and user definable function keys.

The obvious challenge is in placing all of these extra functions within the reach of the average hand. Sometimes the designers have been successful, and sometimes they have failed dramatically. The worst failures—as illustrated by the Atari 800—are when new keys have displaced the old, with resulting confusion and inconvenience for all.

Check These Keys

For word processing purposes, the location of the following keys will prove essential: the cursor control keys, the control key (labelled **ctrl**) and the escape key (labelled **esc**). The Xerox 820 has pioneered by putting its control keys next to the space bar, where they are easily reached with either hand. By contrast, the Televideo 912 has only a single control key that must be contacted by the left little finger, without being mistaken for the tab, alpha lock, or shift key with which it is in close proximity.

The Televideo's most dangerous feature is the location of its block conversion key just below the shift key. This key allows the terminal to be used for editing off-line. Should it be pressed by accident, easy enough given its awkward location, you may lose a half-hour's editing.

Choosing the Terminal

Though you can pay up to $5,000 for a video terminal, one costing between $700 and $1,000 is adequate for the needs of an office of one to three individuals. The basic video terminal is the Lear Siegler ADM 3 which provides the following desirable features

> • an addressible cursor which allows full use of the screen, not just a line at a time,

> • upper and lower case letters and symbols.

Neither the Apple II nor the TRS-80 Model 1 provide these features.

You will want a fully addressible cursor, and the software to make use of it, in order to edit the entire contents of the screen at one time. If your applications include order entry, or the completion of other standard forms, you may want a more expensive terminal like the Televideo 912C which provides protected fields, reverse video (black on white) underline and flashing displays to highlight a particular area.

Additional features offered by more expensive terminals such as extra-cost 'function keys' will duplicate features your word processing software will provide. You do not need to pay for them twice. However, you may find some features of the more expensive models worth paying for. The Televideo 950 offers the following advantages over the Televideo 912C:

> • special graphics' characters

> • more dots per character, 14x10

> • tiltable screen

> • detached keyboard

The ADDS Esprit has one invaluable feature, usually found only on terminals costing $2,500 and more—a nonglare, non-smear screen. This is another feature which may not sell itself at first reading, but which is indispensible when you are looking for day-in day-out performance from yourself and your staff.

Buy Service First

Don't forget a hidden feature—service. Xerox and Radio Shack owners should always find service close at hand. Televideo owners may obtain service from any GE Instrument Service Center. Establish the availability of service in your area before you buy any component.

CHECK LIST

VIDEO TERMINAL FEATURES

THE KEYBOARD

1. Standard typewriter keyboard

    • correct feel

    • numbers, punctuation marks in correct locations

    • indented key tops

    • positive action

2. All keys within easy reach

    • shift keys

    • ctrl key

    • cursor controls and home key

    • delete key

3. Optional features

    • alphabet only shift key

    • detachable keyboard

    • numeric key pad

• programmable function keys

THE SCREEN

1. Easy on the eyes

   • overhang or recessed screen

   • glare-free screen

   • smear-free screen

   • contrast/brightness controls easy to reach

   • reverse video (optional

   • amber/green (optional)

   • tilt/swivel base (optional)

2. Lots of editing room

   • 24 lines

   • status line (optional)

   • 80 characters per line

   • 132 characters per line (optional)

   • screen width 12" or more

3. Easy to read

   • more dots per character

   • lower case descenders, check your g's and q's

   • graphics (optional)

THE COMMUNICATIONS INTERFACE

1. Control codes

    • works with the software you want to buy

2. Data transfer rate

    • variable from 300 to 9600 baud

    • 19.2 kbaud or greater (optional)

3. Communications control keys

    • easy to access

4. Interfaces

    • two RS232C

    • one parallel (optional)

CHAPTER 12

Choosing a Printer

Choosing a printer for your word processor will require an intricate series of tradeoffs in speed, legibility, and price. You'll want 1) flexibility in materials—will it handle forms, labels, and typing paper? and 2) reliability in service—who will maintain it? Your key to a successful investment is a thorough understanding of your application.

Non-Impact Printers

Your first decision in choosing a printer is to decide among impact and non-impact devices. The non-impact printers are the most desirable from the point of view of maintenance. Wear and tear is minimal since there is no actual contact or 'impact' with the paper.

At present non-impact printers are either too expensive or the quality is inferior. At the bottom end of the scale are the thermal printers. These make sense when they are part of a hand-held calculator or a portable terminal like a Texas Instrument 767. They have no place in the office. A salesman may offer to throw one in as 'part of a system.' The AppleSilentype is frequently 'given away' in this manner. Take the money.

At the top of the quality and price range, a laser printer from Xerox can deliver photographic quality at lightning speed for just under $100,000. Last year, the least expensive ink-jet printer cost $25,000. The week I wrote this chapter, a four-color ink-jet printer for under $6,000 was announced. By this time, who knows?

Should you wait for the new models? No! New models of printers are like new models of cars. Let someone else work the bugs out. And beware of software lag. It may be six months to a year before the software is available that will let you take advantage of a new model's features.

Five years from today, the ink-jet printer, a non-impact printer, will be part of every desk-top system. For now, make do with an impact printer and a nearby repairman.

Impact Printers

Impact printers can be subdivided into line versus character printers, as well as dot-matrix versus fully formed character. A line printer prints a line—80 to 132 characters— at a time, and from 1 to 10 lines per second. You'll need the speed of a line printer to support an office with three or more professionals.

Line printers are expensive. But all hard copy devices are expensive once you include all the options. These options include a uni- or bi-directional tractor feed for continuous forms, a form feeder for single sheets (they can cost more than the printer itself), and a speed upgrade. With hard copy devices, you get exactly what you pay for. To be sure you don't buy more than you need, **know your application before you buy.**

Character-by-character printers may be subdivided into 'daisy wheel' (or letter quality) and 'dot matrix.' A step before the daisy wheel are the various adapters you can buy to turn an electric typewriter into a printer. The results will have letter quality, but you'll find a typewriter just isn't fast enough to keep up with the output from your new word processing system.

Dot matrix printers are less expensive than daisy wheels, and "almost" letter quality. These printers form each letter from a matrix of dots, typically five rows by seven columns. The quality of individual letters can vary from fuzzy to unrecognizable. A recent innovation is the two-pass dot-matrix printer. The second pass overlays the first one, providing somewhat better quality. But the quality still falls short of the professional.

Other Factors

Other factors essential to your selection include reliability, as measured by mean time between failures, and software availability. There is no point in paying extra for special features if you haven't got the programs to make use of them. Incidentally, most word processing software is available in

Spinwriter, Qume and Xerox/Diablo versions. Do not consider any other printer, unless it has compatible control codes.

Compatibility, Flexibility, and Service

Would you buy an automobile if you weren't sure of the availability of service? Be equally cautious about a prospective printer. Remember, it has more mechanical parts than any other component of a word processing system.

Be sure that the printer you buy can handle all the forms you use each day: single sheets (both letter and ledger widths), continuous forms, and labels. Refer to the check list of applications you completed before you buy.

CHOOSING A PRINTER
YOUR NEEDS
AND YOUR OPTIONS

Printer Type	Print Quality	Cost	Speed	Reliability	Features
Thermal	poor	low	moderate	high	portability
Typewriter adaptor	good	medium low	slow	varies	familiar keyboard
Dot-matrix	fair	moderate	medium fast	varies	good for graphics
Daisywheel	good	medium	medium	good	widely used
Thimble	good	medium	medium	better	NEC only
Line	poor to good	medium high	fast	better	used with big computers
Ink-Jet	best	medium high to high	fast to very fast	improving	could be the wave of the future

Tentative choices 1. _____

2. _____

CHAPTER 13

Selecting the Computer for Your Word Processor

Selecting the computer and the mass storage devices for your word processor will require a number of decisions on your part. In this chapter, we review the alternatives and provide the background you need to make a series of informed decisions. We give you the information, but the choices are up to you.

Buy Your Own? Or Share a Computer?

If you are hesitant about investing in a word processor, you can get your feet wet through an inexpensive personal computer time-sharing service like CompuServe or the Source. You pay $15 per hour to CompuServe in prime time, for example, to share the resources of their mainframe DEC-10 computer. You will need to buy, rent, or lease some equipment. But you can use this equipment as part of your own word processing system, should you decide to press ahead with the investment at a later date.

The equipment you'll need includes a video or a printer terminal, and a telephone modem to link the terminal to a telephone line.

You can use a video terminal (about $650 to $1,150 retail) to send an electronic mailgram to any CompuServe subscriber anywhere in the United States. CompuServe is prepared to support full screen editing with some models of video terminal, and only line-by-line editing with others. Ask the timesharing service you're considering for a current listing of compatible terminals before you make your selection.

If you want hardcopy, you'll need a printer terminal with an RS232C interface, retailing for about $3,000. (If you are doing price comparisons be sure to compare the keyboard/send/receive (KSR) models of each brand.) Since the printer terminal has a keyboard, you can use it as an electric typewriter when you aren't connected to the time-sharing service.

Dedicated Word Processor or Desk-Top Computer?

The idea that you can buy a complete word processing system for less than $7,000 may still seem strange to you. After all, salesmen from Lanier, NBI, and Wang have been calling at your office for months now trying to sell you a dedicated word processor for $12,000 or $15,000 or more. Dedicated systems whose base price is lower, like IBM's Displaywriter and the Wangwriter, will still cost over $10,000 once you add a second disk drive and a letter-quality printer.

The distinction between a dedicated word processor and a desk-top computer is that the dedicated processor is sold as an integrated system designed specifically for word processing. A desk-top may be purchased component by component, and in most cases you will purchase the computer and the word processing software separately.

The extra money for a dedicated word processor may be worth paying in one instance—when you need to see your text displayed on the screen exactly as it will appear in print. The dedicated word processors manufactured by CPT (Minneapolis, MN) and NBI (Boulder, CO) can display subscripts and superscripts, and Greek as well as Latin symbols.

NBI equipment can also provide:

- automatic kerning

- automatic indenting of paragraphed material

- automatic numbering and indenting of tables of contents.

NBI equipment can provide continuous backup to disk through the use of an independent disk controller. But at least one user complained this backup feature could backfire; during a thunderstorm it is possible to destroy the text on disk as well as the text in memory.

We found that almost every other feature of the dedicated word processor can be matched or exceeded by the right combination of desk-top computer hardware and software. In a survey of spelling checkers, for example, we found three software packages for desk-tops that beat anything dedicated word processors could offer.

Finally, 'dedicated' can mean 'inflexible.' The dedicated word processors can provide data processing capability only through expensive, over-priced add-on's. Unless you work routinely with mathematical equations or chemical formula, we think you'll find the desk-top a best-buy.

Hobbyist? or Professional Quality?

There have been ten times as many hobbyist computers like the Apple and the TRS-80 Model I sold as all other brands of desk-tops combined. The reason is the price. A manager of a small unit in a corporation can usually fit an Apple into his budget, particularly if he buys it a component at a time. The $5,000 plus cost of most professional quality desk-tops may require a second or even a third signature for approval.

Professional quality machines are to be preferred for their reliability, their quality and their expansion capabilities. Atari disk drives are notorious for destroying disks. The normal video display of the Apple or Atari is only 40 characters wide. If you are planning on a multiuser, multiterminal system, your choice has already been made: you must purchase a professional quality system.

Yet, there are many, many positive features to the Apple and the recently introduced TRS-80 Model III that can make a hobbyist computer attractive even to the professional.

First, software is plentiful. Software developers for hobbyist computers know there is a substantial market for their products. We looked at over 24 word processing packages for the Apple, for example.

Second, Apples and Ataris have superb graphics capability. With modest enhancements to existing software, Apples and Ataris could provide a feature offered by only the most expensive dedicated word processors—the ability to display text on the screen exactly as it will appear in print, subscripts, superscripts, Greek symbols and all.

Third, Apples are portable. Only one professional quality system, the Osborne I, also offers portability. An aluminum carrying case that will fit under an airplane seat is included in the Osborne's purchase price. The Osborne's $1,795 price tag also includes some $1,200 worth of software.

Fourth, and perhaps a decisive factor, is service. Apple and Radio Shack dealers are everywhere. If you go with a professional quality CP/M based system, you may need repairs less frequently, but, with a few notable exceptions, the service may not be there when you need repairs.

The exceptions are the new professional systems offered by traditional office equipment suppliers like IBM, Victor Business Products, and Xerox. We consider these systems and more under the heading 'professional quality systems.'

Which Hobbyist System?

Recently, I published a head-to-head comparison of the various hobbyist systems (excluding the Atari) in *Computer Shopper* magazine. I put the Apple first, the TRS-80 second, and the Pet last. I was deluged with complaints from TRS-80 owners demanding to know why their computer wasn't rated h igher. I did not receive a single letter from Pet owners. The silence says more than a thousand letters could.

I chose the Apple over the TRS-80 and two TRS-80 look-alikes, the PMC-80 and the LNW-80, because the Apple has more software, more graphics capability, and more independent service outlets. I'll confess to a personal bias against Tandy products because I've had so many bad experiences with the service and reliability of their stereo components. One Tandy computer, the Model II, must be distinguished from the rest, and I propose the Model II as a professional quality alternative in the next section.

To do word processing on an Apple, you'll have to buy an upper/lower case chip ($35-$70), and an 80-column board ($200-$400). The normal Apple display is upper case only and just 40 columns wide. Two recently introduced word processors—The Word Handler and SuperScribe II, can provide upper/lower case capability and an 70 column display without hardware modification.

In any event, you'll have to buy a video monitor to go with the Apple ($179 up). The home TV, which many hobbyists use for games, provides too fuzzy an image for editing text.

The TRS-80 Model III needs no modifications. It is ready to go as delivered with upper/lower case and an 80-column video display. You'll have your choice of two excellent full-screen word processing packages—Scripsit from Radio Shack, and Electric Pencil from LJG publications.

The Atari can match the Apple for graphics capability. It offers upper and lower case built-in. But its shift key is one silly little centimeter to the right of where an experienced typist would expect it to be. There are three full-screen editors for the Atari—Text Wizard from DataSoft, Letter Perfect from LJK (who also sell a version for the Apple), and WPS (from Atari). None offers all of the features of the weakest of the Apple word processors.

Professional Quality Systems

In order of annual sales, the leading desk-top systems offering professional quality are:

1. The TRS-80 Model II

2. Intertec (or Superbrain)

3. The IBM-PC

4. The North Star Horizon

5. Zenith/Heath

This ranking is changing with the recent entry into the desk-top market place of such traditional office suppliers as Moore Business Systems, Victor Business Products and Xerox. There are also some 45 to 50 other alternatives including Altos, AVL Eagle, Durango, Dynabyte, Exidy, Icom, Kontron, Onyx, Pertec, Quay, and Rair.

WARNING: With 135 or more brands on the market, and more entering every day, competitive elimination of some of these brands is inevitable. Choose with care. Buy service first. If you can't get service locally for a unit, forget it. And ask yourself whether this service will be available a few years from now.

8-bit or 16-bit?

A feature most professional quality systems have in common is their use of one of the family of 8-bit 8080 computer chips and of the 8080 based CP/M operating system. The use of a common operating system has the advantage of making software developed for use on one brand of computer readily adaptable for use on another.

Two major manufacturers, IBM and Victor Business Products, have elected to use the 16-bit 8088 (or 8086) computer chip in their desk-top computers, the IBM DisplayWriter and Personal Computer, and the Victor 9000. These computers offer roughly four times the throughput of the more common 8-bit desk-top for certain applications.

The 16-bit capacity offers no particular advantage for word processing. However, the graphics capability of these machines makes them worth a second look. In the works, for example, is a 16-bit version of Spellbinder designed for use on the Victor 9000 that will display proportional spacing on the screen as it appears in print. When used with the appropriate keyboard, it will display accents and vowels for French and Arabic.

Tables 7 and 8 in the appendix are devoted to head-to-head comparisons of the 16-bit word processing software.

How Much Mass Storage?

Much like automobiles, each professional quality brand of desk-top has several models. The difference between models is mainly in the amount of mass storage and in the type of mass storage device—hard disk or floppy disks, 5 1/4" inch or 8" floppies. You don't need a hard disk for word processing; it is far too expensive for the application. You will need at least two floppy disk drives, however, one for the program and one for your files.

You will probably prefer 5 1/4" disks to 8" disks for word processing on the basis of both convenience and price. You can store more letters on a large disk, but smaller disks make it simpler to keep files organized. (A good analogy is the file folder.)

If you purchase 5 1/4" disk drives with most off-brands of CP/M-based computers, you will find your selection of software quite limited. That's because the only uniform standard among computers that use the CP/M operating system is for single-density 8" drives. You'll avoid this problem if you let your software choose your computer.

The amount of mass storage on disk will depend upon the following factors:

- diameter of the disk

- density

- number of sides

- computer operating system

Photo courtesy of Quay Corp.

Hard disk drive and floppy disk drive in the same chassis.

The Xerox 820 can hold 84 thousand characters—
that's about 8 times the length of this chapter—on each
of its one-sided, single-density 5 1/4" drives. The Quay
500 can hold 200 thousand characters on each of its one-
sided, double-density 5 1/4" drives. The Quay 540 can hold
800 thousand characters on each of its two-sided, quad-
density 5 1/4" drives.

Actually, we wouldn't recommend either the Xerox or
the Quay for word processing. The storage capacity of the
Xerox 820 is too limited. The Quay is an off-brand; though
its wood grain cabinet marks it as executive quality, it is
just too difficult to get software and service for it.

The Operating System

The operating system normally does its work behind the
scenes, communicating with the video terminal and the
printer, maintaining directories of disk files, and positioning
the read head on the disk. The operating system will also
determine what applications software you can run on your
computer. Rule 1 again: **choose your software first; let
your software choose your operating system.**

Apple and Radio Shack owners have their choice of at
least three categories of operating systems. The owners
of other brands of computer are not so fortunate, and may
find their choices in applications software more limited.
Here are the principal operating system choices:

• TRSDOS

• AppleDOS

• UCSD Pascal

• Oasis

• CP/M

• CP/M 86

• MS DOS

As the acronym suggests, TRSDOS is specific to Tandy Radio Shack equipment and is included in the purchase price of each Radio Shack system. Three full-screen word processors will run under TRSDOS compatible operating systems—Scripsit, Newscript, and Electric Pencil.

There are two versions of AppleDOS, both included in the price of Apple equipment. One is specific to the Apple II and one to the Apple III. Some fifteen or more full-screen word processors will run on the Apple II under AppleDOS. But these same word processors will not run on the Apple III.

UCSD Pascal may be ignored for word processing purposes although PowerText, a very powerful printer formatter for the IBM-PC, makes use of the UCSD Pascal text editor and operating system. The one advantage of UCSD Pascal over other operating systems is its portability. Its use will permit totally disparate computers like the 8-bit Apple II and the 16-bit LSI-11 to exchange files and programs.

Oasis is a multiuser operating system. A variant of one of the best printer formatters available on IBM mainframe computers—Waterloo Script, is also available under Oasis.

Versions of CP/M run on over 70 makes of computers including the TRS-80 Model I and the Apple II after suitable hardware modifications. Over 30 word processing packages run under CP/M.

Operating Systems for 16-bit Computers

CP/M-86 and MS-DOS are standard operating systems on the new 16-bit 8088/86 desktops like the IBM-PC, the DEC Rainbow, and the Victor 9000. Most of the traditional CP/M based word processors, such as Benchmark and WordStar, have been redesigned for use under the CP/M-86 operating system. Spellbinder makes use of MS-DOS, as do a variety of brand new word processors including EasyWriter 2.0 and Volkswriter.

At press time, an operating system had not yet been settled on for the 68000 based 16-bit Radio Shack Model 16. Probably, it will use a variant of the Unix system originated by Bell Laboratories. Unfortunately, the presence of yet another operting system can only compound the problems of software selection. The best protection for you, the consumer, is to follow out very first rule: *Select your software first; let the application determine the hardware.*

CHECK LIST

SELECTING A COMPUTER

Before you select a computer for your word process-ing system, force yourself to answer all the following questions. These questions must be answered if you are to make an intelligent buying decisions.

1. Your own computer?   ————
    or   ————
    A time sharing terminal   ————
2. Dedicated word processor?   ————
    or
    A desk-top computer?   ————
3. A hobbyist computer?   ————
    or
    A professional quality desk-top?   ————
4. Single user?   ————
    or
    Multi-user system?   ————
5. How much mass storage do you need?   ————

Let your software choose your computer.

List your first three choices in word processing software.

1. ————

2. ————

3. ————

Which operating system is best for your needs?

for word processing _____

for other data processing _____

Make a list below of the models that satisfy your needs. Eliminate those that cannot be serviced locally.

BRAND	MODEL	SERVICE	PRICE

PART 4

THE DECISION

CHAPTER 14

The Best Word Processor

My staff is often asked for the name of the one *best* word processor. Our invariable answer is "what is best will depend upon your application." In this chapter we consider some of the common applications for "author, lawyer, merchant chief." If the shoe doesn't quite fit, make a close examination of the comparison tables at the end of this book to find the word processor that is best for you.

Author

Most authors have one clear goal—to get their ideas down on paper as quickly and as accurately as possible before the ideas slip away. They dream of being able to type and type without once having to look back to see if it was typed correctly. The word processor has been the author's liberator. Authors are now free to progress in two steps. First the ideas, and then the corrections. And when they are finished, magically, there is not an erasure on the paper. Obviously, publishers benefit from the clean copy that is submitted.

I have found Magic Wand now called Peach Text essential in my role as an author, primarily because of its file control capabilities. Peach Text makes it easy to borrow a paragraph or two from earlier articles. I can edit one file, display a second, and insert a third, even though each of the files is stored on a different disk. Numerous safeguards in the Peach Text software reduce the likelihood of destroying my own work. But Peach Text's printer formatter has drawbacks.

Lawyer

Attorneys who make efficient use of their time build on previous efforts. Once a paragraph has been drafted with sufficient care to ensure that the rights of one client are protected, it may serve equally well to protect the rights of another. Building a will or a contract is more than a matter of combining the right paragraphs, of course. To the degree the repetitive insertion of standard paragraphs and boiler plate is automated, the attorney is freed to focus on the individual aspects of each case.

Attorneys need a word processor that will allow them to merge sections from several files. They want a word processor that will require minimum involvement of their staff. They should be able to print multiple copies and several documents in a row with a single command. Peach Text, Spellbinder, and SuperText all lend themselves to this application. SuperText has a split screen editing feature that the others do not. Spellbinder's extensive formatting capabilities provide for generating line numbers in the margins of a document.

Merchant Chief

Merchant chiefs are characterized by at least three attributes (most of which they share in part with all the other professions):

> • There is a wide range of documents for which they are responsible—correspondence, mailing lists, reports, and accounts.

> • They delegate preparation of these documents to others.

> • They are concerned with numbers as much as they are with words.

Since most tasks will be delegated to subordinate personnel, it is important that the word processing software be self-documenting and include optional help menus. (Reliance upon a single 'knowledgeable' individual is suicidal. You want a system that can be used—at least the easier features—by even temporary employees.) Select, for example, has excellent documentation and help menus.

The preparation of ledger sheets is outside the range of most word processors. Exceptions are Typemaster and Word Star which permit horizontal scrolling, allowing the user to work with a 132-character document on an 80-character wide video screen. And either may be used to interchange columns as well as rows in the ledger.

Even if you own a electronic spread sheet like SuperCalc or VisiCalc, you'll find a word processor the ideal way to <u>underline headings</u> or add **Bold** face for emphasis. Incidentally, SuperText (for the Apple) has a built-in electronic worksheet, though its horizontal scrolling capability is limited to alternating left and right 40 column windows.

Physician

In most instances, the word processing needs of physicians and dentists are secondary to the medical billing function. Though a limited word processing capability is part of many medical billing packages, you may want to shop around if you plan extensive use of a word processor. WARNING: Don't buy a word processor unless it is compatible with the software and hardware you already own.

A further essential is a good spelling checker, particularly one that will allow you to create your own medical dictionary. See Chapter 9 on spelling checkers for recommendations.

Programmer

Programmers' needs were considered in Chapter 8 on extra software features. Best bets are Perfect Writer for CP/M-based computers or SuperText for the Apple. While several word processors can be modified to work with programs as well as text (see tables) only Perfect Writer and SuperText will allow the simultaneous display of new and old versions of a program side by side.

Publisher

This book stems in part from our own lengthy search for the 'ideal' word processor to help us with our publishing needs. We prepare three newsletters each month for research laboratories, physicians, and time-sharing users respectively, and we need all the help we can get in automating the editing and formatting processes.

Spellbinder lends itself to the editing process. It's possible for an editor to insert comments so they are displayed on the screen in an intensity distinct from the original author's. As a result, both the editor and the author feel freer in inserting corrections, and experimenting with alternate ways of saying things.

Spellbinder is also our first choice for printer formatting. It can get the most from any letter-quality printer. Working from a menu, one can adjust the space between lines to the nearest 1/48th of an inch and the space between characters to the nearest 1/120th of an inch. Spellbinder and Scripsit are the only programs that provide for printing multiple columns with a single pass of the printer. The alternative of reversing the line-feed at the end of the first column is far slower and far less reliable. Printers and uni-directional tractor feeds are notorious for jamming or skipping a line when they are thrown into reverse.

Although most word processors *claim* a proportional spacing capability—in which the lower case "j", for example, takes up a fraction of the room required by an uppercase "M"—Newscript and Spellbinder are the only programs to give us effective control over the proportional spacing features of our own printer, the C. Itoh.

CHAPTER 15

Using the Comparison Tables to Select a Text Editor

We evaluated over forty text editors, but not all of them made it to the comparison tables at the end of this book. We eliminated several editors we felt were promising because they were not widely available. Private label variants of text editors included in the tables were also eliminated. An example is Wordsworth distributed by Leading Edge, which is an enhanced version of Magic Wand, adapted for use on a Zenith/Heath terminal.

Once word of our project leaked out, we received a rather bizarre collection of manuals and software for review. If we couldn't read the manual, we couldn't and didn't review the software. In some instances, when a totally illegible manual bore the proud legend "edited and formatted on our own word processor," we did draw certain tentative conclusions.

We eliminated text editors that did not allow us to make full use of the video screen. These included line-by-line editors, and editors that took up so much of the screen with help menus that there was no room left for the text. And finally, we eliminated those text editors which in the opinion of our staff were too slow in execution for practical business use.

Guide to the Tables

We evaluated each text editor on the basis of 82 criteria, some of which we elaborate on below. I hope you will find the comments helpful when you use the evaluation tables.

Overall

Years on the market is a reflection of a product's maturity. With time, there is opportunity for revision and correction, and, hopefully, for improvement.

Four of the criteria are unique to the Apple. These include:

1. **Backup.** To forestall software pirates, Apple software is often provided in noncopyable form. Unfortunately, floppy disks are all too mortal. Their lifetime can vary from six months to six seconds. You should always have a backup on hand. Most Apple word proces-

sors come with a backup disk. Beware of those that don't.

2. **Upper/Lower Case** and a **Greater than 40 Column Screen.** The Apple seems inexpensive at first glance but that is because its base price does not include many of the features that are standard on more expensive brands of computer. The normal display provides upper case only and a mere 40 columns. While this is adequate for games, it frustrates business applications. There are two solutions. The first is hardware-oriented and entails the purchase of an upper/lower case chip, and an 80-column display board ($300 to $500 for both). With this approach, you need software that can take advantage of these hardware features.

3. **Hi-Res Graphics.** A far better solution, also unique to the Apple, takes advantage of the Apple's high-resolution graphics to generate a completely new character set. Only two of the word processors in our study, both newly released, have taken this approach. They are Screenwriter II and Word Handler, and they offer a 70-column upper and lower case display without hardware assist.

Other Important Features

Menus make it easy to start using a new system, but if they need to be accessed every time, they will get in the way of the more experienced user.

Displays of *multiple files* facilitate the side-by-side review of two versions of a program or a document.

The printer is the slowest component of a word processing system. The ability to *display* the text on the

screen as it will appear in print can reduce the time required to prepare a document by up to fifty percent. The
ability to *print* one file while editing a second can give you
the power of a second computer.

Control Characters. It is easier to learn a new system
when its control characters can be altered to those of a
more familiar system. But look for trouble when more than
one version is in use at one time.

You'll need to handle files *larger than memory* when
you write a book, or integrate several quarterly reports into
a single annual summary.

Documentation

You will need at least two types of documentation: tutorials
to get you started, and reference material when you want
a quick refresher course. You'll find examples, sample
files, and help menus to be essential in either case. A
separate quick-reference card that can be propped up by
your terminal is indispensable.

File Control

File control is the guts of any word processing system.
You'll want all of the control features listed in the comparison table.

Continuous Backup (so you don't lose your copy during a power failure). Continuous backup is not a feature of
most desk-top word processors, unfortunately. *Save a File*
and continue editing is next best. Make it a habit to back
up after each page. Keep a backup of the original though,
in case you change your mind about the changes.

You need *safeguards.* The system should warn you if you try to save a file on top of a file with the same name. The system should automatically *backup* each edit with a copy of the pre-edit file.

A disk will hold only so much information. If a disk is full, you won't be able to save a file you've just created or changes you've just made, unless you can *kill* an existing file to make space.

You'll want to *insert* or *display* material from earlier files; the fewer commands it takes to do it, the better. You'll need to display the file *directory* to help in remembering the names of existing files.

Prepare Files for Transmission

The threat of software piracy has caused some Apple and Atari software developers to overprotect their wares with little regard for user convenience. As a result, you may not be able to prepare files for transmission over telephone lines. A "no" in this row of the table may be fatal to your application.

Full-Screen Editors

The principal advantage of the full-screen editor is that it provides the end-user with the luxury of an electronic tablet. You scroll rapidly through a document, a word or a sentence at a time, or jump to the beginning or end of the text. Some word processors may limit your scrolling abilities to the beginning or end of the workspace. *Horizontal Scrolling* will let you work with documents that are wider than the screen display.

Delete. You'll want to delete entire phrases, as well as letter by letter. Look for safeguards. Avoid the risk of deleting material you have no intention of deleting.

Insert Options

You can use all five of the following ways to insert text:

- prestored phrases

- typeover

- an insert mode for complete phrases

- a push-ahead mode for inserting just a few characters or words

- a block mode for moving or copying blocks of text

We've found splitting and gluing a line at a time, or using an intermediate buffer to be far too time-consuming.

Search and Replace

All the text editors we reviewed could find a phrase and replace it with another automatically, but not all would

- pause after each occurrence to give the option to retain or replace

- replace more than one occurrence of a phrase with a single command

- replace all occurrences with a single command

• scan an entire document, when the document was larger than memory.

Using a *Wild Card* to stand for an arbitrary letter or series of letters can simplify your editing chores in three situations:

• First, when you can't remember how to spell the word you are looking for, as in Smith, Smyth, or Sm?th

• Second, when you want to find all occurrences, whether Smith, Smith's or Smit?

• Third, when typing it all out is too much of a chore, as in Sm? instead of Smithsonian

Screen Format

Displaying the text on the screen as it will appear in print can save you up to fifty percent of the time you'd normally spend in formatting a document. Adjustable line length is important. Using the full width of the screen is best when first entering a text. Using a short line of about 50 characters is best when you are reviewing and making changes. The best way to set tabs is with the *cursor,* just as if you were using a typewriter. But setting *tabs by command* is better than not having tabs at all.

Using the Tables

Some of the above features will strike you as essential to your application. Others won't be as relevant. Go through the comparison tables at the end of this book and highlight the essential features in red. Eliminate any word processor that cannot provide those features.

CHAPTER 16

Selecting a Printer Formatter

You can enhance the appearance of your programs and reports with the aid of a printer formatter. A good formatter will provide you with maximum control over the appearance of your printed output while minimizing the need for your personal intervention.

All the word processors listed in our text editor comparison tables include printer formatters with the exception of Vedit. Unfortunately, a good text editor may be accompanied by a bad printer formatter. Shop with care. You may want to consider buying a second word processor or a pure printer formatter like Scribble or TextWriter.

A discussion of the criteria used in our formatter comparison tables is included below.

Saving Your Time

The ability to display a document on the screen exactly as it will appear in print can reduce the time required to prepare a document for final printing by as much as fifty percent. You can experiment with different margin settings, indents, and single and double spacings. Experimenting at the video terminal is an order of magnitude faster (and less noisy) than experimenting on a printer.

Remarkable time-savings can also be achieved when your formatter allows you to:

• print one file while editing another

• merge files, like an address file and a form letter.

Few formatters can support all the special features of every printer, not when each new model of printer provides more features than the one before. There is a definite software lag. Most formatters can support at least three of the following four "standard" printers:

• Centronics 737

• Diablo

• NEC

• Qume

Other printers will adhere to one or the other of these standards. For example, the C. Itoh printer uses Qume control codes. To avoid problems, follow the rule of choosing your software first; let your software determine your choice of printer.

Four Sets of Features

A formatter should be evaluated on the ease and flexibility with which it provides control over page layout, spacing and pagination, the printer, and the printing process.

Page Layout and Page Control

There are two approaches to formatting a text; one using a *menu*, the other *embedded commands*. The two approaches are not mutually exclusive. The best text formatters allow you to do both, and, moreover, to *interrupt* while a document is printing and further modify the format.

Optimally, a text formatter should allow you to set up *multiple headings and footings*, with *automatic pagination* and an *odd/even* page distinction. It should provide for a *conditional new page*, overriding the preset layout, if a single line or phrase would be left isolated at the bottom or top of a page.

Spacing and Pagination

Right or left *justification*, and automatic *centering* of one or more lines of text are provided by almost all text formatters. Scribble, from Mark of the Unicorn, goes farther than any other formatter in providing for a total environment of spacing, centering, and indenting with a single command.

Phantom or *soft-hyphens* are a text-formatting time saver. You can't afford the time to rehyphenate a text each time you delete a word or alter a line length. Peach Text has this feature.

Multiple columns and *reverse line feeds* are luxury options required only if you act as your own publisher or have specialized applications. Spellbinder from Lexisoft can provide multiple columns with a single printer pass. Other formatters require you to invest in a bi-directional tractor feed.

Printer Enhancements

Underlining and **bold face** are provided by every text formatter we reviewed. Only a few formatters allow the user to *vary* the degree of boldness. Still fewer permit both underlining and bold face in a single line of print. Palantir is one of the few to provide for combinations of enhancements.

Kerning is a printer's trick designed to cram one or two extra letters on a given line, by reducing the space allotted to each. You'll need it only for specialized applications.

Proportional spacing is more of a necessity; you'll find it makes text look more attractive, and allows you to get more words per page in an easy-to-read format. But beware; even the best text formatters support proportional spacing with only a few print styles. Check for compatibility before you buy.

Output Control

Again we remind you that a good printer formatter minimizes the need for user intervention yet allows for full user interaction. Look for the ability to

> • Interrupt then resume printing, in order to change a type face, or to leave to answer the telephone. (An unattended printer is not a good idea.)

> • Enter text from the keyboard to add a personal postscript to a form letter.

> • Start or stop at a designated page or record.

> • Print multiple copies or multiple documents with a single command.

PART 5

COMPARISON TABLES

TABLE 1: Comparison of CP/M Text Editors

CP/M TEXT EDITOR	Bench mark	Memorite III	Palantir	Peach text
	$499	$399	$299	$500
OVERALL				
years on market	2	2	>1	3
for all CP/M based computers	no	Vector Gr	yes	yes
menu driven	yes	no	yes	no
can display multiple files	no	no	no	no
displays text on screen				
as it will appear in print	yes	yes	yes	no
handles files larger than memory	yes	no	yes	yes
can edit programs as well as text	yes	no	yes	yes
control characters can be customized	no	no	hard	yes
DOCUMENTATION				
getting started	easy	easy	hard	easy
tutorials	good	confusing	yes	excel
examples	some	many	some	many
help menus	many	many	yes	some
reference material	no index	good	poor	good
separate reference card	no	no	lengthy	yes
FILE CONTROL				
continuous back-up	yes	no	no	no
save file and continue editing	no	no	yes	yes

automatic back-up on file save	yes	yes	yes	yes
file replace safeguards	yes	yes	yes	yes
insert a second file with one command	yes	yes	append	no
insert a portion of a second file	yes	no	no	yes
display a second file	no	yes	yes	yes
display file directory	yes	yes	yes	yes
kill file (and create space)	yes	yes	yes	yes
can prepare files for transmission	yes	yes	yes	yes
SCROLLING (or cursor movement)				
by word	yes	no	yes	yes
by line	yes	yes	yes	yes
by sentence	no	no	yes	no
by screen	yes	yes	yes	yes
to beginning or end of workspace	yes	no	yes	yes
to beginning or end of document	hard to do	no	yes	no
horizontal scroll	yes	no	yes	no
DELETE				
by character	yes	yes	yes	yes
by word	yes	yes	yes	no
by line	yes	yes	yes	yes
by sentence	no	yes	yes	no
by screen	yes	no	yes	no
by block	slow	yes	yes	yes
continuous delete	yes	no	yes	no
block delete safeguards	no	no	yes	yes

CP/M TEXT EDITOR	Bench mark	Memorite III	Palantir	Peach Text
INSERT				
phrases inserted with single key	52	none	36	none
typeover (fast)	yes	yes	yes	yes
insert mode (fast for several lines)	yes	no	no	yes
push ahead (fast for 1 or 2 letters)	no	yes	yes	yes
split and glue a line at a time	no	no	no	no
intermediate buffer	via disk	no	yes	no
block whole sections	via disk	yes	slow	yes
move columns	yes	no	no	no
delete and restore	slow	no	no	no
SEARCH				
find phrase anywhere in document	yes	no	slow	no
find with user option to replace	yes	yes	yes	no
find and replace n times	no	yes	yes	yes
find and replace all in document	yes	no	slow	no
find and replace all in memory	yes	yes	yes	yes
use wild cards	yes	yes	yes	no
ignore upper/lower case in matching	yes	yes	yes	yes
SCREEN FORMAT				
format entire text	yes	yes	yes	no
format different parts differently	yes	no	yes	no
set line length	yes	yes	yes	yes
set tabs with cursor	yes	yes	yes	no
set tabs by command	no	no	no	yes

TABLE 1: Comparison of CP/M Text Editors continued

CP/M TEXT EDITOR	Perfect Writer	Select	Spell-binder	Type-Master	Vedit	Word Star
	$289	$595	$495	$400	$130	$445
OVERALL						
years on market	<1	2	3	1	2	3
for all CP/M based computers	yes	yes	yes	yes	yes	yes
menu driven	yes	yes	no	no	no	yes
can display multiple files	yes	no	no	no	no	no
displays text on screen as it will appear in print	no	yes	yes	yes	no	yes
handles files larger than memory	yes	no	yes	yes	yes	yes
can edit programs as well as text	yes	no	yes	yes	yes	yes
control characters can be customized	yes	no	yes	yes	yes	no
DOCUMENTATION						
getting started	good	best	easy	easy	hard	hard
tutorials	good	good	good	some	poor	good
examples	several	none	not enough	few	none	some
help menus	yes	yes	yes	no	no	yes
reference material	good	excel	good	some	fair	excel
separate reference card	yes	yes	no	no	no	yes
FILE CONTROL						
continuous back-up	yes	no	no	yes	no	no
save file and continue editing	yes	yes	yes	no	yes	yes

CP/M TEXT EDITOR	Perfect Writer	Select	Spell-binder	Type-Master	Vedit	Word Star
FILE CONTROL continued						
automatic back-up on file save	no	yes	yes	yes	no	yes
file replace safeguards	no	no	yes	no	yes	yes
insert a second file with one command	yes	yes	yes	yes	no	yes/no
insert a portion of a second file	yes	no	no	no	no	yes/no
display a second file	yes	no	yes	no	no	no
display file directory	yes	yes	yes	if full	no	yes
kill file (and create space)	yes	yes	yes	yes	no	yes
can prepare files for transmission	yes	yes	yes	yes	yes	yes
SCROLLING (or cursor movement)						
by word	yes	no	yes	yes	no	yes
by line	yes	no	yes	yes	yes	yes
by sentence	yes	no	yes	no	no	yes
by screen	yes	yes	yes	yes	yes	yes
to beginning or end of workspace	yes	no	yes	yes	yes	yes
to beginning or end of document	yes	no	yes	no	no	yes
horizontal scroll	no	no	yes	yes	no	yes
DELETE						
by character	yes	no	yes	yes	no	yes
by word	yes	no	yes	no	no	yes
by line	yes	no	yes	yes	yes	yes
by sentence	yes	no	yes	no	no	no
by screen	no	no	no	no	no	no
by block	yes	yes	yes	yes	no	yes

continuous delete	no	no	no	no	no
block delete safeguards	yes	yes	no	no	yes
INSERT					
phrases inserted with single key	none	40	none	none	none
typeover (fast)	yes	yes	no	no	yes
insert mode (fast for several lines)	no	yes	no	yes	yes
push ahead (fast for 1 or 2 letters)	yes	no	yes	yes	yes
split and glue a line at a time	no	no	yes	no	no
intermediate buffer	no	yes	no	no	no
block whole sections	no	yes	hard	yes	yes
move columns	no	yes	yes	no	yes
delete and restore	yes	yes	no	no	no
SEARCH					
find phrase anywhere in document	no	yes	yes	yes	yes
find with user option to replace	yes	yes	no	no	yes
find and replace n times	no	yes	no	no	yes
find and replace all in document	no	yes	no	no	yes
find and replace all in memory	yes	yes	no	no	no
use wild cards	no	yes	no	no	yes
ignore upper/lower case in matching	yes	yes	yes	no	yes
SCREEN FORMAT					
format entire text	no	yes	yes	no	yes
format different parts differently	no	view mode	yes	no	yes
set line length	no	yes	yes	no	yes
set tabs with cursor	no	yes	yes	no	yes
set tabs by command	yes	yes	no	yes	yes

TABLE 2: Comparison of CP/M Printer Formatters

CP/M PRINTER FORMATTER	Bench mark	Memorite III	Palantir	Peach Text
OVERALL				
display on screen as it will print	yes	yes	yes	yes
mail-merge or file-merge	yes	yes	xtra $	yes
almost all printers supported	not Qume	yes	yes	yes
conditional formats	yes	no	xtra $	yes
footnotes	—	5 per pg	no	no
LAYOUT				
set from a menu	yes	yes	yes	yes
menu may be skipped	yes	yes	yes	yes
under user control while printing	yes	yes	yes	yes
characters per inch	yes	yes	yes	yes
lines per inch	yes	yes	yes	partial
width limitation	155	none	none	none
PAGE CONTROL				
one line heading	yes	yes	yes	yes
multi-line heading	yes	yes	yes	yes
heading and footing	yes	yes	yes	yes
page numbering	yes	yes	yes	yes
odd, even page distinction	yes	yes	yes	no
conditional new page	no	no	yes	yes

TEXT CONTROL				
justify	yes	yes	yes	yes
center	yes	yes	yes	yes
phantom hyphen	no	yes	yes	yes
multiple columns	no	yes	yes	yes
reverse line feed	no	yes	yes	yes
PRINTER CONTROL				
underline	yes	yes	yes	yes
bold face	yes	yes	yes	yes
vary bold face intensity	no	no	yes	yes
super- and sub-script	yes	yes	yes	yes
change ribbon colors	no	no	yes	no
kerning	no	yes	no	yes
change control characters	no	no	yes	yes
proportional spacing	no	yes	yes	partial
OUTPUT CONTROL				
interrupt, resume	no	yes	yes	yes
alter format	no	no	yes	yes
pause for text entry from keyboard	no	yes	yes	yes
pause for variable entry	no	yes	xtra $	yes
start, stop at designated page, record	yes	yes	yes	yes
print multiple documents	yes	yes	yes	no
print multiple copies	no	yes	yes	yes

145

TABLE 2: Comparison of CP/M Printer Formatters continued

CP/M PRINTER FORMATTER	Perfect Writer	Select	Spell-binder	Type-Master	Vedit	Word Star
OVERALL						
display on screen as it will print	yes	yes	yes	yes		yes
mail-merge or file-merge	no	no	yes	yes		$130 extra
almost all printers supported	not Qume	almost	yes	some	Text editor only	yes
conditional formats	yes	no	hard to do	yes		no
footnotes	yes	no	no	yes		(option)
LAYOUT						
set from a menu	no	yes	yes	no		yes
menu may be skipped	no	no	yes	yes		no
under user control while printing	yes	no	yes	yes		yes
characters per inch	yes	yes	yes	hard to do		yes
lines per inch	yes	no	yes	hard to do		yes
width limitation	none	132	none	none		none
PAGE CONTROL						
one line heading	yes	yes	yes	yes		yes
multi-line heading	yes	yes	yes	no		no
heading and footing	yes	yes	no	yes		yes
page numbering	yes	yes	yes	yes		yes
odd, even page distinction	yes	no	yes	no		yes

	Col 1	Col 2	Col 3	Col 4	Col 5
conditional new page	yes	yes	hard to do	no	yes
TEXT CONTROL					
justify	yes	yes	yes	yes	yes
center	yes	yes	yes	yes	yes
phantom hyphen	no	yes	yes	no	no
multiple columns	no	yes	yes	no	yes
reverse line feed	no	no	yes	no	yes
PRINTER CONTROL					
underline	yes	yes	yes	yes	yes
bold face	yes	yes	yes	yes	yes
vary bold face intensity	yes	no	yes	no	yes
super- and sub-script	yes	yes	yes	yes	yes
change ribbon colors	no	no	yes	no	yes
kerning	yes	no	yes	no	no
change control characters	yes	no	yes	no	no
proportional spacing	hard	yes	yes	yes	no
OUTPUT CONTROL					
interrupt, resume	yes	yes	yes	yes	yes
alter format	no	no	yes	yes	yes
pause for text entry from keyboard	yes	no	hard to do	yes	yes
pause for variable entry	yes	no	hard to do	yes	yes
start, stop at designated page, record	no	yes	yes	yes	yes
print multiple documents	yes	no	yes	yes	no
print multiple copies	yes	yes	yes	yes	yes

TABLE 3: Comparison of Apple II Text Editors

APPLE TEXT EDITOR	Apple Writer $75	Easy Writer $129	Easy Writer Pro $259	Letter Perfect $150
OVERALL				
years on market	3	2	1	3
back-up	one	no limit	no limit	by mail
works with upper/lower case	print only	no	yes	yes
works with 80 column screen	no	no	yes	yes
uses Hi:Res graphics	no	no	no	no
menu driven	no	yes	yes	no
can display multiple files	no	yes	yes	no
displays text on screen as it will appear in print	no	no	no	no
handles files larger than memory	no	no	no	no
can edit programs as well as text	yes	no	no	no
control characters can be customized	no	no	no	no
DOCUMENTATION				
getting started	slow	slow	slow	fair
tutorials	good	puerile	puerile	fair
examples	no	no	one	one
help menus	some	yes	yes	no
reference materials	good	fair	fair	good
separate reference card	yes	no	yes	yes

	1	2	3	4
FILE CONTROL				
continuous back-up	no	no	no	no
save file and continue editing	yes	yes	yes	yes
automatic back-up on file save	no	no	no	no
file protect safeguard	no	no	no	no
insert a second file with one command	yes	yes	no	yes
insert a portion of a second file	no	no	no	no
display a second file	no	no	no	no
display file directory	yes	yes	yes	yes
kill file (and create space)	no	yes	yes	yes
can prepare files for transmission	yes	yes	no	yes
SCROLLING (or cursor movement)				
by word	no	no	no	no
by line	yes	yes	yes	yes
by sentence	no	no	no	no
by screen	yes	yes	yes	yes
to beginning or end of workspace	yes	yes	yes	yes
to beginning or end of document	no	no	no	no
horizontal scroll	no	no	no	no
DELETE				
by character	yes	yes	yes	yes
by word	no	no	no	yes
by line	no	yes	yes	yes
by sentence	no	no	no	prgrph
by screen	no	no	no	no
by block	yes	yes	yes	no
block delete safeguard	yes	no	no	no
continuous delete	no	no	no	no

APPLE TEXT EDITOR

	Apple Writer	Easy Writer	Easy Writer Pro	Letter Perfect
INSERT				
keyphrases	none	none	none	none
typeovers (fast)	yes	yes	yes	yes
insert mode (for many words)	no	no	no	no
push ahead (for one or two letters)	yes	yes	yes	no
split and glue a line at a time	no	yes	yes	no
intermediate buffer	no	hard	hard	no
block whole sections	no	no	yes	no
delete and restore	yes	no	yes	yes
SEARCH				
find phrase anywhere in document	no	no	yes	no
find with user option to replace	yes	no	yes	yes
find and replace n times	no	no	no	no
find and replace all in document	no	no	yes	no
find and replace all in memory	yes	no	yes	no
use wild card	yes	no	no	no
ignore upper/lower case in matching	no	yes	yes	no
SCREEN FORMAT				
format entire text	no	no	yes	no
format different parts differently	no	no	no	no
set line length	no	no	yes	no
set tabs with cursor	no	no	no	yes
set tabs by command	no	no	yes	no

TABLE 3: Comparison of Apple II Text Editors continued

APPLE TEXT EDITOR	Magic Window $100	Pie Writer $130	Screen Writer $130	Super Text $150	Word Handler $189	Word Star $375
OVERALL						
years on market	2	>1	>1	2	>1	1
back-up	no	unlimited	by mail	one	one	no limit
works with upper/lower case	yes	yes	yes	yes	yes	yes
works with 80 column screen	no	yes	yes	no	66	yes
uses Hi-Res graphics	no	no	yes	no	yes	no
menu driven	no	no	yes	no	no	yes
can display multiple files	no	no	yes	no	no	yes
displays text on screen as it will appear in print	yes	no	partial	no	yes	yes
handles files larger than memory	no	no	yes	yes	no	yes
can edit programs as well as text	yes	yes	yes	no	no	yes
control characters can be customized	no	no	yes	no	no	no
DOCUMENTATION						
getting started	excel	easy	fair	hard	good	hard
tutorials	fair	good	fair	minimal	poor	good
examples	no	yes	several	few	none	some
help menus	no	yes	yes	needed	none	yes
reference materials	fair	good	fair	poor	poor	excel
separate reference card	yes	yes	yes	yes	yes	yes

APPLE TEXT EDITOR	Magic Window	Pie Writer	Screen Writer	Super Text	Word Handler	Word Star
FILE CONTROL						
continuous back-up	no	no	no	no	no	no
save file and continue editing	no	yes	no	yes	no	yes
automatic back-up on file save	no	no	no	no	no	yes
file protect safeguard	no	no	no	yes	no	yes
insert a second file with one command	yes	no	no	yes	yes	yes
insert a portion of a second file	yes	no	no	no	yes	yes
display a second file	no	no	no	yes	no	yes
display file directory	yes	yes	yes	yes	no	yes
kill file (and create space)	no	yes	no	yes	no	yes
can prepare files for transmission	yes	yes	yes	no	yes	yes
SCROLLING (or cursor movement)						
by word	no	yes	yes	no	yes	yes
by line	no	yes	yes	yes	yes	yes
by sentence	no	no	no	no	no	yes
by screen	yes	yes	yes	yes	yes	yes
to beginning or end of workspace	yes	yes	yes	yes	yes	yes
to beginning or end of document	no	no	no	yes	no	yes
horizontal scroll	yes	partial	no	no	no	yes
DELETE						
by character	yes	yes	yes	yes	yes	yes
by word	no	yes	no	yes	yes	yes
by line	yes	yes	yes	yes	yes	yes

by sentence	no	no	no	no	no	no
by screen	no	no	no	yes	yes	no
by block	no	yes	yes	yes	yes	yes
block delete safeguard	no	yes	yes	no	no	yes
continuous delete	no	no	no	no	no	no
INSERT						
keyphrases	none	none	none	"the"	none	none
typeovers (fast)	no	yes	yes	yes	yes	yes
insert mode (for many words)	no	no	yes	no	yes	yes
push ahead (for one or two letters)	no	yes	no	yes	no	yes
split and glue a line at a time	yes	yes	no	no	no	no
intermediate buffer	no	yes	yes	no	yes	no
block whole sections	no	no	no	yes	no	yes
delete and restore	yes	no	no	no	no	no
SEARCH						
find phrase anywhere in document	no	no	no	yes	no	yes
find with user option to replace	no	no	yes	yes	yes	yes
find and replace n times	no	no	yes	no	no	yes
find and replace all in document	no	no	no	yes	no	yes
find and replace all in memory	no	limited	yes	yes	no	no
use wild card	no	no	yes	yes	no	yes
ignore upper/lower case in matching	no	no	yes	yes	no	yes
SCREEN FORMAT						
format entire text	yes	no	yes	no	yes	yes
format different parts differently	yes	no	yes	no	no	yes
set line length	yes	no	yes	no	yes	yes
set tabs with cursor	yes	yes	no	no	yes	yes
set tabs by command	yes	yes	yes	no	no	yes

TABLE 4: Comparison of Apple II Printer Formatters

APPLE PRINTER FORMATTER	Apple Writer	Easy Writer	Easy Writer Pro	Letter Perfect
OVERALL				
display on screen as it will print	no	yes	yes	no
print one file while editing another	no	no	no	no
mail-merge or file-merge	no	xtra $	xtra $	xtra $
almost all printers supported	no	yes	yes	yes
LAYOUT				
set from a menu	no	no	yes	no
menu may be skipped	no	no	yes	no
under user control while printing	no	no	no	no
characters per inch	no	yes	yes	yes
line per inch	no	no	no	yes
width limitation	80	125	125	80
PAGE CONTROL				
one line heading	yes	yes	yes	yes
multi-line heading	no	no	yes	no
heading and footing	no	no	yes	yes
page numbering	no	yes	yes	yes
odd/even page distinction	no	no	no	no
conditional new page	no	no	no	no

154

TEXT CONTROL

justify	yes	yes	yes	yes
center	yes	yes	yes	yes
phantom hyphen	no	no	no	no
conditional formats	no	no	no	no
multiple columns	no	no	no	no
reverse line feed	no	no	no	no

PRINTER CONTROL

underline	xtra $	yes	yes	yes
bold face	xtra $	yes	yes	yes
vary bold face intensity	xtra $	hard	hard	no
super- and sub-script	no	yes	yes	yes
change ribbon colors	no	no	no	no
kerning	no	yes	yes	no
change control characters	no	yes	yes	no
proportional spacing	no	no	yes	yes

OUTPUT CONTROL

interrupt/resume	no	no	no	no
pause for text entry from keyboard	no	no	no	no
pause for variable entry	xtra $	no	no	no
start/stop at designated page/record	no	no	no	no
print multiple documents	no	yes	yes	no
print multiple copies	xtra $	no	no	yes

TABLE 4: Comparison of Apple II Printer Formatters continued

APPLE PRINTER FORMATTER	Magic Window	Pie Writer	Screen Writer	Super Text	Word Handler	Word Star
OVERALL						
display on screen as it will print	yes	no	yes	yes	no	yes
print one file while editing another	no	no	yes	no	no	slow
mail-merge or file-merge	no	no	yes	xtra $	no	xtra $
almost all printers supported	no	no	yes	yes	yes	yes
LAYOUT						
set from a menu	no	no	yes	yes	yes	yes
menu may be skipped	no	no	no	yes	no	no
under user control while printing	no	yes	yes	no	no	yes
characters per inch	no	no	yes	no	yes	yes
line per inch	no	no	yes	no	yes	yes
width limitation	80	132	none	127	132	none
PAGE CONTROL						
one line heading	no	yes	yes	no	yes	yes
multi-line heading	no	no	4 lines	no	no	yes
heading and footing	no	yes	yes	no	yes	yes
page numbering	yes	yes	yes	yes	yes	yes
odd/even page distinction	no	no	no	no	yes	no
conditional new page	no	yes	yes	no	auto	yes

TEXT CONTROL						
justify	yes	yes	yes	no	yes	yes
center	yes	yes	yes	yes	limited	yes
phantom hyphen	no	no	yes	no	no	no
conditional formats	no	no	no	no	no	no
multiple columns	no	no	no	no	no	yes
reverse line feed	no	no	no	no	no	no
PRINTER CONTROL						
underline	no	yes	yes	yes	yes	yes
bold face	no	no	yes	yes	yes	yes
vary bold face intensity	no	no	no	yes	no	yes
super- and sub-script	no	no	yes	yes	yes/no	yes
change ribbon colors	no	no	no	yes	no	yes
kerning	no	no	no	no	no	no
change control characters	no	no	yes	yes	no	no
proportional spacing	no	no	yes	yes	no	yes
OUTPUT CONTROL						
interrupt/resume	no	no	yes	yes	no	yes
pause for text entry from keyboard	no	yes	yes	no	no	yes
pause for variable entry	no	no	yes	no	yes	yes
start/stop at designated page/record	yes	yes	yes	no	no	yes
print multiple documents	no	yes	yes	yes	no	yes
print multiple copies	no	no	yes	yes	no	yes

TABLE 5: Comparison of TRS-80 Text Editors

TRS-80 TEXT EDITOR	Electric Pencil II $175	Newscript	Scripsit I $299	Scripsit II $399
OVERALL				
years on market	3	2	2	1
for Radio Shack Models	I,III	I,III	I,III	II
menu driven	in part	no	yes	yes
can display multiple files	no	no	no	no
displays text on screen as it will appear in print	no	no	yes	yes
handles files larger than memory	no	no	yes	yes
can edit programs as well as text	yes	yes	no	no
control characters can be customized	yes	no	no	no
DOCUMENTATION				
getting started	easy	easy	slow	slow
tutorials	good	wordy	good	best
examples	no	some	many	many
help menus	yes	no	yes	yes
reference material	good	excel	fair	fair
separate reference card	yes	yes	no	yes
FILE CONTROL				
continuous back-up	no	yes	yes	yes
save file and continue editing	no	yes	yes	yes

automatic back-up on file save	no	no	no	no
file replace safeguards	no	no	no	no
insert a second file with one command	yes	yes	yes	yes
insert a portion of a second file	yes	no	no	no
display a second file	no	no	no	no
display file directory	yes	yes	yes	yes
kill file (and create space)	yes	yes	yes	yes
can prepare files for transmission	yes	yes	yes	yes
SCROLLING (or cursor movement)				
by word	yes	yes	no	no
by line	yes	yes	no	no
by sentence	no	no	yes	yes
by screen	yes	yes	yes	by page
to beginning or end of workspace	yes	yes	yes	yes
to beginning or end of document	yes	no	yes	yes
horizontal scroll	yes	no	no	yes
DELETE				
by character	yes	yes	yes	yes
by word	no	yes	yes	yes
by line	yes	no	no	no
by sentence	no	yes	yes	yes
by screen	no	no	no	no
by block	yes	yes	yes	yes
continuous delete	no	no	no	no
block delete safeguards	yes	no	yes	yes

159

TRS-80 TEXT EDITOR	Electric Pencil	Newscript	Scripsit I	Scripsit II
INSERT				
phrases inserted with single key	no	none	none	20
typeover (fast)	yes	yes	yes	yes
insert mode (fast for several lines)	no	yes	yes	yes
push ahead (fast for 1 or 2 letters)	yes	yes	no	no
split and glue a line at a time	no	yes	no	no
intermediate buffer	no	no	no	no
block whole sections	yes	yes	yes	yes
delete and restore	no	no	no	no
SEARCH				
find phrase anywhere in document	yes	yes	yes	yes
find with user option to replace	yes	no	no	yes
find and replace n times	yes	yes	yes	yes
find and replace all in document	no	no	yes	yes
find and replace all in memory	yes	yes	yes	yes
use wild cards	yes	no	no	no
ignore upper/lower case in matching	no	no	no	yes
SCREEN FORMAT				
format entire text	no	no	yes	yes
format different parts differently	no	no	yes	yes
set line length	no	no	yes	yes
set tabs with cursor	no	no	yes	yes
set tabs by command	no	no	yes	yes

TABLE 6: Comparison of TRS-80 Printer Formatters

TRS-80 PRINTER FORMATTER	Electric Pencil II	Newscript	Scripsit I	Scripsit II
OVERALL				
display on screen as it will print	no	partial	yes	yes
print one file while editing another	no	no	no	yes
mail-merge or file-merge	no	yes	no	yes
almost all printers supported	partially	yes	many	many
conditional formats	no	yes	no	no
LAYOUT				
set from a menu	yes	no	yes	yes
menu may be skipped	no	—	yes	yes
under user control while printing	no	yes	no	no
characters per inch	difficult	yes	yes	yes
lines per inch	difficult	yes	yes	yes
width limitation	no	no	80	156
PAGE CONTROL				
one line heading	yes	yes	yes	yes
multi-line heading	no	6 lines	yes	yes
heading and footing	no	yes	yes	yes
page numbering	yes	yes	yes	yes
odd/even page distinction	no	no	no	no
conditional new page	no	yes	no	no

TRS-80 PRINTER FORMATTER	Electric Pencil II	Newscript	Scripsit I	Scripsit II
TEXT CONTROL				
justify	yes	yes	yes	yes
center	no	yes	yes	yes
phantom hyphen	no	no	no	no
multiple columns	no	no	no	yes
reverse line feed	no	no	no	yes
PRINTER CONTROL				
underline	yes	yes	yes	yes
bold face	hard to do	yes	yes	yes
vary bold face intensity	hard to do	no	no	no
super- and sub-script	no	yes	yes	yes
change ribbon colors	yes	no	no	no
kerning	yes	yes	no	no
change control characters	no	no	no	yes
proportional spacing	no	yes	no	no
OUTPUT CONTROL				
interrupt, resume	yes	yes	no	yes
alter format	yes	no	no	no
pause for text entry from keyboard	no	yes	no	no
pause for variable entry	no	yes	no	no
start/stop at designated page/record	no	yes	yes	yes
print multiple documents	no	yes	no	no
print multiple copies	yes	yes	yes	yes

TABLE 8: Comparison of Atari Text Editors

ATARI TEXT EDITOR	Atari WP	Letter Perfect $150	Text Wizard $129
OVERALL			
years on market	1	1	1
back-up	no	$20 by mail	$5 by mail
uses Hi-Res graphics	no	no	no
menu driven	yes	yes	no
can display multiple files	no	no	no
display text on screen	yes	no	no
as it will appear in print	yes	no	no
handles files larger than memory	yes	no	no
can edit programs as well as text	no	no	yes
control characters can be customized	no	no	no
DOCUMENTATION			
getting started	slow	slow	easy
tutorials	hopeless	no	no
examples	yes	none	none
help menus	cumbersome	no	no
reference material	cumbersome	yes	good
separate reference card	yes	yes	yes

ATARI TEXT EDITOR	Atari WP	Letter Perfect	Text Wizard
FILE CONTROL			
continuous back-up	by page	no	no
save file and continue editing	yes	yes	yes
automatic back-up on file save	no	no	no
file protect safeguard	yes	yes	no
insert a second file with one command	yes	yes	yes
insert a portion of a second file	no	no	no
display a second file	no	no	no
display file directory	no	yes	yes
kill file (and create space)	no	yes	yes
can prepare files for transmission	no	no	yes
SCROLLING (or cursor movement)			
by word	no	no	no
by line	yes	yes	yes
by sentence	no	no	no
by screen	yes	yes	yes
to beginning or end of workspace	yes	yes	yes
to beginning or end of document	yes	no	no
horizontal scroll	yes	no	no
DELETE			
by word	yes	no	no
by line	yes	yes	yes

by sentence	no	no	no
delete recover	yes	no	no
by screen	yes	no	no
by block	yes	yes	yes
block delete safeguard	no	yes	no
continuous delete	no	yes	no
INSERT			
keyphrases	no	no	no
typeovers (fast)	yes	yes	yes
insert mode (for many words)	no	no	yes
push ahead (for one or two letters)	yes	yes	yes
split and glue a line at a time	no	no	no
intermediate buffer	yes	yes	no
block whole sections	complex	no copy	yes
delete and restore	yes	yes	no
SEARCH			
find phrase anywhere in document	yes	not appl	not appl
find with user option to replace	yes	yes	yes
find and replace n times	no	no	no
find and replace all in document	yes	no	no
find and replace all in memory	yes	no	no
use wild cards	no	no	no
ignore upper/lower case in matching	no	no	no

ATARI TEXT EDITOR

	Atari WP	Letter Perfect	Text Wizard
SCREEN FORMAT			
format entire text	yes	no	no
format different parts differently	no	no	no
set line length	yes	no	no
set tabs with cursor	no	yes	no
set tabs by command	yes	no	no

TABLE 7: Comparison of Atari Printer Formatters

ATARI PRINTER FORMATTER	Atari WP	Letter Perfect	Text Wizard
OVERALL			
display on screen as it will print	yes	no	no
print one file while editing another	no	no	no
mail-merge or file-merge	no	xtra $	xtra $
letter quality printers supported	no	no	no
LAYOUT			
set from a menu	yes	no	no
menu may be skipped	yes	—	—
under user control while printing	no	no	no
characters per inch	yes	yes	yes
lines per inch	no	no	no
width limitation	80	80	80
PAGE CONTROL			
one line heading	yes	yes	yes
multi-heading	no	no	no
heading and footing	no	yes	yes
page numbering	yes	yes	yes
odd/even page distinction	yes	no	no
conditional new page	yes	no	no

ATARI PRINTER FORMATTER

	Atari WP	Letter Perfect	Text Wizard
TEXT CONTROL			
justify	yes	yes	yes
center	yes	yes	yes
phantom hyphen	no	no	no
conditional formats	no	no	no
multiple columns	yes	no	yes
reverse line feed	no	no	no
PRINTER CONTROL			
underline	yes	yes	yes
bold face	yes	yes	yes
vary bold face intensity	no	no	no
super- and sub-script	yes	yes	yes
change ribbon colors	no	no	no
kerning	no	no	yes
change control characters	no	no	no
proportional spacing	yes	yes	yes
OUTPUT CONTROL			
interrupt/resume	no	no	no
pause for text entry from keyboard	no	no	no
pause for variable entry	no	no	no
start/stop at designated page/record	yes	yes	yes
print multiple documents	no	no	yes
print multiple copies	no	yes	no

TABLE 9: Comparison of IBM-PC Text Editors

IBM-PC TEXT EDITOR	Benchmark	EasyWriter IBM	EasyWriter IUS	Power Text	Vedit	Volks Writer
OVERALL						
back-up	no	no	no	yes	yes	no
menu driven	yes	yes	yes	yes	no	one
can display multiple files	no	no	no	no	no	no
displays text on screen						
as it will appear in print	yes	no	yes	no	no	no
handles files larger than memory	yes	no	yes	no	yes	no
can edit programs as well as text	yes	yes	yes	yes	yes	yes
control characters can be						
customized	no	yes	yes	no	yes	no
DOCUMENTATION						
getting started	hard	O.K.	good	fair	hard	easy
tutorials	good	poor	sparse	good	no	on-line
examples	no	2	3	many	no	many
help menu	yes	o.k.	good	o.k.	no	one
reference material	no index	yes	good	good	no index	sparse
separate reference card	no	yes	yes	no	no	no
FILE CONTROL						
continuous back-up	by page	no	by page	no	no	no
save file and continue editing	no	no	yes	yes	yes	yes
automatic back-up on file save	yes	no	no	no	no	no
file replace safeguards	yes	no	no	no	yes	no

IBM-PC TEXT EDITOR	Benchmark	EasyWriter IBM	EasyWriter IUS	Power Text	Vedit	Volks Writer
FILE CONTROL continued						
insert a second file with one command	yes	no	no	yes	yes	yes
insert a portion of a second file	no	append	yes	yes	yes	yes
display a second file	no	yes	no	no	no	no
display file directory	yes	no	no	no	no	no
kill file (and create space)	yes	no	no	no	yes	no
can prepare files for transmission	yes	yes	yes	yes	yes	yes
SCROLLING (or cursor movement)						
by word	yes	yes	yes	no	yes	yes
by line	yes	yes	yes	no	yes	yes
by sentence	no	no	yes	no	no	no
by screen	yes	yes	no	yes	no	yes
to beginning or end of workspace	yes	yes	yes	yes	yes	yes
to beginning or end or document	hard to do	no	yes	no	yes	no
horizontal scroll	yes	yes	yes	no	yes	no
DELETE						
by character	yes	yes	yes	yes	yes	yes
by word	yes	yes	yes	no	no	yes
by line	yes	yes	no	yes	yes	yes
by sentence	no	no	no	no	no	no
by screen	yes	no	no	no	no	no
by block	yes	yes	yes	yes	hard	yes
continuous delete	yes	yes	yes	yes	no	yes
block delete safeguards	no	yes	yes	yes	no	no

INSERT

phrases inserted with single key	52	no	no	no	no	no
typeover (fast)	yes	yes	yes	yes	yes	yes
insert mode (fast for several lines)	yes	yes	no	yes	no	yes
push ahead (fast for 1 or 2 letters)	no	yes	yes	yes	yes	yes
split and glue a line at a time	no	yes	no	yes	no	yes
intermediate buffer	via disk	yes	yes	yes	yes	no
block whole sections	via disk	yes	yes	yes	hard	yes
move columns	yes	no	no	no	no	no
delete and restore	slow	yes	no	yes	no	no

SEARCH

find phrase anywhere in document	yes	yes	no	no	no	no
find with user option to replace	yes	yes	yes	yes	no	yes
find and replace n times	no	no	no	yes	yes	no
find and replace all in document	yes	yes	no	no	no	no
find and replace all in memory	yes	yes	yes	yes	yes	yes
use wild cards	yes	no	no	no	yes	no
ignore upper/lower case in matching	yes	yes	no	no	yes	no

SCREEN FORMAT

format entire text	yes	yes	yes	yes	no	no
format different parts differently	yes	yes	yes	yes	yes	yes
set line length	yes	yes	yes	yes	no	yes
set tabs with cursor	yes	no	no	no	no	yes
set tabs by command	no	yes	yes	yes	yes	no

TABLE 10: Comparison of IBM-PC Printer Formatters

IBM-PC PRINTER FORMATTER	Benchmark	EasyWriter IBM	EasyWriter IUS	Power Text	Vedit	Volks Writer
OVERALL						
display on screen as it will print	yes	yes	yes	no	Text editor only ———————	yes
mail-merge or file-merge	xtra $	no	no	yes		yes
almost all printers supported	yes	yes	yes	yes		yes
conditional formats	no	no	no	no		no
footnotes	unlimited	no	no	no		no
LAYOUT						
set from a menu	yes	yes	yes	no		yes
menu may be skipped	yes	no	no	no		yes
under user control while printing	yes	no	no	no		no
characters per inch	yes	yes	yes	yes		yes
lines per inch	yes	yes	yes	yes		yes
width limitation	none	no	no	none		none
PAGE CONTROL						
one line heading	yes	yes	yes	yes		no
multi-line heading	yes	yes	yes	yes		no
heading and footing	yes	yes	yes	yes		no
page numbering	yes	yes	yes	yes		yes
odd/even page distinction	no	yes	yes	yes		no
conditional new page	yes	no	n.a.	no		n.a.

	1	2	3	4	5
TEXT CONTROL					
justify	yes	yes	yes	yes	yes
center	yes	yes	yes	yes	yes
phantom hyphen	yes	no	no	no	no
multiple columns	no	no	no	yes	no
reverse line feed	no	no	yes	no	no
PRINTER CONTROL					
underline	yes	yes	yes	yes	yes
bold face	yes	yes	yes	yes	yes
vary bold face intensity	yes	no	no	yes	no
super- and sub-script	yes	yes	yes	yes	no
change ribbon colors	no	no	yes	no	no
kerning	no	no	no	no	no
change control characters	no	yes	yes	yes	no
proportional spacing	no	no	no	yes	no
OUTPUT CONTROL					
interrupt, resume	yes	yes	yes	no	yes
alter format	yes	no	no	no	no
pause for text entry from keyboard	xtra $	no	no	no	no
pause for variable entry	xtra $	no	no	no	no
start/stop at designated page/record	yes	no	yes	no	yes
print multiple documents	yes	yes	yes	no	yes
print multiple copies	yes	no	yes	no	no

Appendix 1

Check List for Contract Negotiations

1. HARDWARE SPECIFICATIONS

   Make, model number

   Number and kind of disk drives

   Amount of formatted mass storage

   Prices

2. SOFTWARE SPECIFICATIONS

   Operating system (free?)

   Text editor

   Printer formatter

3. INSTALLATION

    Guaranteed delivery date

    Make payment contingent

    on complete and successful

    installation of all hardware

    and software

4. TRAINING

    When?

    How soon after installation?

    Number of Hours

    Location(s)

5. MAINTENANCE

    Length of warranty

    Extent of coverage

        parts

        labor

        office calls

        loaners

        guaranteed turn-around

Appendix 2

Check List of Miscellaneous Needs

- CORDS AND CABLES

  RS232C for video terminal

  Amphenol connector for printer

- FLOPPY DISK

  number of 10 packs _____

  disk holder

- FURNITURE

  typist chair (armless)

  two-shelf stand for disk drives

  and CRT (height adjustment)

  printer table (has paper-feed slot in top)

  (acoustic insolation for printer)

  static-control mat

• MODEM for telephone

  direct-connect

  300, (1200) baud

  (auto-dial/auto-answer)

• POWER supply

  multiply outlet power strip

  surge suppressor

  line-noise suppressor

  backup power supply

• PRINTER supplies

  print wheels (3 minimum)

  ribbons

  form feeder

  single sheets

  envelopes

  labels

Appendix 3

A Time-Saving Device

Users with a heavy volume of correspondence or reports can literally double their productivity with a $325 hardware printer spooler, the SmartBuffer, from Data Match. In some offices, where the desk-top is used primarily for word processing, both the micro and the employees may be tied up all afternoon printing out the morning's work. That was certainly the case in my office while we were producing this book. The SmartBuffer gives control of your computer back to you.

Here is how it works: The SmartBuffer acts as a buffer, talking to the micro at computer speed (9600 Baud). It can store 5 to 40 pages of text (16K to 128K RAM). The SmartBuffer feeds the printer at the slower printer speed (300 to 1200 baud) until the work is done. This leaves your computer completely free for other tasks—more reports, financial modeling, or manpower assignment.

A general ledger which tied up your computer every Friday morning is no longer a problem. You can easily make hard copies of all your graphic displays which typi-cally require 10 to 15 minutes each to reproduce.

A variety of hardware spoolers are available vary-ing in capacity, price, ease of use, and flexibility. The

SmartBuffer and the SuperSpooler stand out in their ability to accept output from several computers simultaneously. The obvious application is where you have several terminals but only one letter quality printer. Dual parallel and serial interfaces permit the SmartBuffer or the SuperSpooler to accept simultaneous input from such diverse sources as Apple and North Star micros, and Burrough's minis and mainframes.

VENDOR	MODEL	PRICE	DESCRIPTION
Compulink Longmont CO 80501 (303) 651-2014	SuperSpooler	$350-$500	16-64K bytes, any computer or printer, serial or parallel space compression, reset button, buffer display.
Practical Peripherals 31245 La Baya Dr Westlake Village CA 91362 (213) 991-8200	Microbuffer	$259-$299	8-16K bytes, Apple II only some printers
Data Match 3810 Oakville Industrial Court Doraville GA 30340 (404) 441-0408	SmartBuffer	$325-$899	16-128K bytes, any computer or printer, (up to 4 of each) serial and/or parallel

Appendix 4

Software for
the IBM Personal Computer

Although the first units of IBM's Personal Computer were shipped in October 1981, the software was a long time in coming. Only one word processor was available then. That was Easy Writer 1.0, not one of our favorites. It was soon replaced by Easy Writer 1.1.

No additional word processing software was available until June 1982, when five packages reached the dealer's shelves almost simultaneously, to be followed in subsequent months by eight more. There are the standards—Wordstar, Benchmark, Select, and Vedit—and entirely new products especially written for the PC like Easy Writer 2.0 (related to 1.1 only by marriage—it's an entirely different concept), and Volkswriter.

The PC is multitasking. You can take full advantage of this multitasking feature by choosing a word processor like EasyWriter 2.0 which will let you print one file while editing another. A drawback of the PC is the confusion of operating systems. Some products run under PC-DOS (or MS-DOS as it is also known), and some require CP/M-86. You'll be better off if you *use one operating system to support all your software.*

On the down side, be prepared to sacrifice one of the IBM PC's most desirable features—color. With IBM's monochromatic board and a black and white monitor ($200-$300), you'll get good crisp 7x9 dot characters in a 9x14 matrix. If you go with color, you're limited to 7x7 characters in an 8x8 dot matrix, and you'll need an RGB color monitor ($900 to $1100)—a color T.V. won't do.

Look into the Victor 9000. It has even better resolution (9x12 in a 10x16 matrix) in black–and–white only, keyboard control over brightness and contrast, and a glare-free, smear-free screen that makes it easy to spend long hours at the terminal. Word processing software includes Word Star and Select. Be careful! The latter has been renamed VictorWriter. We tested it and found it took inordinately long to erase a single character like the s in rats.

Seattle Computer Company announced the purchase price of its 16-bit _Gazelle_ would include the MS-DOS operating system and Perfect Writer. Unfortunately, the latter is also not one of our favorite word processors.

Photo courtesy of IBM

IBM's Personal Computer

Appendix 5

Vendors List

WORD PROCESSORS FOR CP/M BASED COMPUTERS

Benchmark	MetaSoft Corporation 711 E Cottonwood Casa Grande AZ 85222 (800) 528-7385	$499	Slow block transfer. Full footnote capability. May not run on all CP/M-based computers.
Final Word Mince Scribble	Mark of the Unicorn P O Box 423 Arlington MA 02174 (617) 489-1387	$300 $175 $175	Word processer. Text editor only. Printer formatter only.
Palantir	Designer Software 3400 Montrose Blv'd Houston TX 77006 (713) 520-8221	$299	From the creators of Magic Wand.
Peach Text (Magic Wand)	Peachtree Software Inc 3 Corporate Square Atlanta GA 30329 (404) 325-8533	$495	Used to prepare this book; formatter has bugs.
Perfect Writer	Perfect Software 1400 Shattuck Ave Berkeley CA 94709 (800) 227-5488	$289	Relative of Mince. User friendly-manual.

Select	Select Information Systems 919 Sir Francis Drake Blvd Kentfield CA 94904 (415) 459-4003	$595	Immature, but very easy to use. Available for NEC.
Spellbinder (Word 125)	Lexisoft, Inc Box 267 Davis CA 95616 (916) 758-3630	$495	Editor and formatter load in single module. Includes file-sort and mail-merge.
Textwriter	Organic Software PO Box 2069 Livermore CA 94550 (415) 455-4034	$125	Text formatter only; does not support proportional spacing.
TypeMaster	ComputerMart 560 West Fourteen Mile Rd Clawson MI 48017 (313) 288-0040	$400	Includes file-sort and mail-merge.
Vedit	Compuview Products 618 Louise Ann Arbor, MI 48103 (313) 996-1299	$145	Text-editor only.
Wordstar	MicroPro 1299 4th Street San Rafael CA 94901 (415) 457-8990	$445	The best-seller.

WORD PROCESSORS FOR THE TRS-80

Electric Pencil II	IJG Inc 1260 W Foothill Blv'd Upland CA 91786 (714) 946-5805	$135	Outdated.
Lazywriter	ABC Sales PO Box 33948 Detroit MI 48232	$125	Excellent manual, lots of extra features.
Newscript	Prosoft Box 560 North Hollywood CA 91603 (213) 764-3131	$125	Proportional spacing; option is $50.
Scripsit	Radio Shack PO Box 2910 Fort Worth TX 76101 (817) 390-3011	$399 $199	For Model II. For Model III.

WORD PROCESSORS FOR THE ATARI

Letter Perfect	LJK Enterprises PO Box 10827 St Louis MO 63129 (314) 846-6124	$150	Not as good as Apple II version.
Text Wizard	DataSoft Inc 19519 Business Center Dr Northridge CA 91324 (800) 423-5916	$99	Good choice for use with CompuServe or The Source.
Word Processor	Atari Inc 1265 Borregas Sunnyvale CA 94086 (800) 538-8543	$150	Manual must have been assembled by a committee.

WORD PROCESSORS FOR THE APPLE

Apple Pie	Hayden Software 50 Essex St Rochelle Park NJ 07662 (201) 843-0550	$130	Versions for every 80 column board.
AppleWriter	Apple Computer Inc Cupertino CA 95014 (408) 996-1010	$75	A best buy.
AppleWriter Extended	Brillig Systems, Inc 10270 Fern Pool Ct Burke VA 22015 (703) 323-1339	$35	Formatting enhancements for AppleWriter.
Easy Writer	Information Unlimited 281 Arlington Ave Kensington CA 94707 (415) 525-9452	$129	Outdated.
Letter Perfect	LJK Enterprises PO Box 10827 St Louis MO 63129 (314) 846-6124	$150	

Magic Window	Softape 10432 Burbank Blvd North Hollywood CA 91601 (213) 985-5763	$100	Best for beginners.
Screenwriter	On-Line Systems 36575 Mudge Ranch Rd Coarsegold CA 93614 (209) 683-6858	$130	New, best buy. Hi-resolution graphics.
Super Text	Muse, Inc 330 N Charles St Baltimore MD 21201 (301) 659-7212	$175	Has built-in calculator.
Word Handler	Silicon Valley Software 652 Bair Island Rd Redwood City CA 94063 (415) 361-1818	$249	Hard to use.
Wordstar	MicroPro 1299 4th Street San Rafael CA 94901 (415) 457-8990	$375	Requires Z-80 card and extra RAM board.

WORD PROCESSORS FOR
THE IBM PERSONAL COMPUTER

Benchmark	MetaSoft Corporation 711 E Cottonwood Casa Grande AZ 85222 (800) 528-7385	$499	Runs under CP/M-86. Block transfer is slow. Full footnoting capability.
Easy Writer 1.1	IBM Box 1328 Boca Raton FL 33432 (305) 998-2000	$175	Over-priced for features.
Easy Writer 2.0	IUS, ltd. 2401 Marinship Way Sausalito CA 94965 (415) 331-6700	$425	Over-priced for features.
Edix/Wordix	Emerging Technology Box 154 Louisville CO 80027 (303) 447-9495	$195/$390	Multiple-file displays. Horizontal scrolling. Requires 128K.

PowerText	Beaman Porter Inc Pleasant Ridge Rd Harrison NY 10528 (914) 967-3504	$399	Full document design with powerful printer formatter; uses Pascal editor. Also Apple III.
Select (VictorWriter)	Select Information Systems 919 Sir Francis Drake Blvd Kentfield CA 94904 (415) 459-4003	$595	Immature; easy to use; can be infuriatingly slow. Runs under CP/M-86.
Volkswriter	Lifetree Software 177 Webster Monterey CA 93940 (408) 659-3221	$195	Easy to use editor. Weak formatter.
Wordstar	MicroPro 1299 4th Street San Rafael CA 94901 (415) 457-8990	$445	The best-seller. Runs under CP/M-86.